THE FORCE
OF CHARACTER

THE FORCE
OF CHARACTER

And the Lasting Life

JAMES HILLMAN

RANDOM HOUSE

NEW YORK

Owing to limitations of space, acknowledgments of permission to quote
from previously published material will be found on page 237.

Library of Congress Cataloging-in-Publication Data
Hillman, James.
The force of character: and the lasting life / James Hillman.
p.   cm.
Includes bibliographical references and index.
ISBN 0-375-50120-7
1. Self-actualization (Psychology) in old age.   2. Character.
3. Adulthood—Psychological aspects.   4. Aged—Psychology.
I. Title.
BF724.85.S45H535   1999b   155.67' 1825—dc21   99-24097

Random House website address: www.atrandom.com
Printed in the United States of America on acid-free paper
24689753
First Edition

Book design by J. K. Lambert

FOR MARGOT,

who never once got on the turtle's case

Old men ought to be explorers.

T. S. Eliot

Contents

A Preface for the Reader

Aging is no accident. It is necessary to the human condition, intended by the soul. Aging is built into our physiology; yet, to our puzzlement, human life extends long beyond fertility and outlasts muscular usefulness and sensory acuteness. For this reason we need imaginative ideas that can grace aging and speak to it with the intelligence it deserves. You will find that vision in this book. It offers the promise of refreshing the reader's mind with a shower of insights whose goal is to affect transitions to later years profoundly, even permanently.

So, why *do* we live so long? Other mammals give way while we go on forty, fifty, sometimes even sixty years beyond menopause. We stay on, lingering in our recliners or marching the treadmill at eighty-eight.

I cannot support the theory that human longevity is the artificial result of civilization, its science and its social networks, yielding a crop of living mummies, paradoxes suspended in a twilight zone. The old as "retards."

Instead, let us entertain the idea that character *requires* the additional years and that the long last of life is forced upon us neither by genes nor by conservational medicine nor by societal collusion. The last years confirm and fulfill character.

—

What human nature most wants to know about human nature is not the chain of development from remotest origins to the immediate now. We want to make some sense of our aging beyond wearing down and running out. What does aging serve? What is its point?

These questions strike suddenly in the midst of living, and not only during the suspiciously American "midlife crisis." That crisis compounds two fears: I am getting on in years, yet am I getting on with what I really am? Aging and character together. This popular syndrome is less about the middle of the life span than about the central crisis of one's nature, less about being too old than about being still too young. Not loss of capacity; loss of illusion.

We will discover more about our midlife crisis by looking critically backward to the sentimental prolongation of adolescence than by focusing upon the nursing home forty years hence. That projection keeps us from being in the midst of life and lays a pall of dread upon the fascinating questions of late life. At forty we are not eighty, and there is far more "awake time" before us than behind. Our midlife encounter with old age is premature. One hasn't the perception yet that can fathom its images, so that the answers one finds in midlife mainly reflect our fears. This book risks very different answers.

To *explain* aging we usually turn to biology, genetics, and geriatric physiology, but to *understand* aging we need something more: the idea of character. Biology is not the body itself, only a way of describing it. Aging is mediated by the stories told about it. Biology tells one kind of story, psychology another. Or, better said, psychology attempts to understand biology's explanations.

Our reality as a living, thinking being comes before our explanations of our living and our thinking. A psychological approach to aging has to stick with this priority. If the idea of soul (even if you can't explain this idea) comes first in value, then our ideas should accord with our actual value system. This means we have to psychologize aging, discover the soul in it.

In the normal course of life, aging ends in dying and our normal thinking about aging draws the same conclusion. If all aging ends in dying, does this mean the whole aim of aging is dying? Biology considers aging as a process leading to uselessness. Rather than a process, let us consider old age as a *structure* with its own essential nature.

Let us ask why our later years take a certain form and show certain characteristics. Perhaps "uselessness" needs to be regarded aesthetically. Must the soul be properly aged before it leaves? We can then imagine aging as a transformation in beauty as much as in biology. The old are like images on display that transpose biological life into imagination, into art. The old become strikingly memorable, ancestral representations, characters in the play of civilization, each a unique, irreplaceable figure of value. Aging: an art form?

———

To make some sense of later years and the often absurd predicaments and ridiculous degradations congruent with age, we do well to return to one of the deepest questions human thought has posed: What is character, and how does it force us into the patterns we live?

What ages is not merely your functions and organs, but the whole of your nature, that particular person you have come to be and already were years ago. Character has been forming your face, your habits, your friendships, your peculiarities, the level of your ambition with its career and its faults. Character influences the way you give and receive; it affects your loves and your children. It walks you home at night and can keep you long awake.

You and I are not the first to face old age, even if we face it for the first time. Humankind has always been aging, so why not draw upon how other people in earlier centuries received it? In our culture this would be a fresh approach. To take our ideas from recent research severely limits our perspectives to what is new—and much of the new will have come and gone by the time this page has been printed and finds its way into your hands. Besides, much of the new originates in denial. An underlying motive in aging research is the drive to get rid of aging, as if it were a cancer.

I, too, am trying to get rid of an idea, or at least shove aside the fixed notion that we are basically physiological creatures and that therefore our thinking about ourselves can be reduced to thinking about our bodies. This notion dooms us; we become victims of aging. We believe our entire existence is yoked to and—most dramatically in later years—governed by physiology.

The idea we are moving in its place says it is to character that you are most truly yoked. "Character," said Heraclitus at the beginning of Western thought, "is fate." No, Napoleon, not geography; and no, Freud, not anatomy, either. Character! Character governs—governing physiology, too. We will be maintaining, with all the heft and perseverance we can still summon, that genetic inheritance is shaped into our own peculiar pattern by character, that specific composition of traits, foibles, delights, and commitments, that identifiable figure bearing our name, our history, and a face that mirrors a "me."

Then we will be able to look at the decay of body and mind as more than affliction. We will connect it with an underlying truth we already feel: Something forms a human life into an overall image, including life's haphazard contingencies and wasted irrelevancies. Later years are often devoted to exploring these irrelevancies, adventuring into past mistakes so as to discover understandable patterns.

The understanding that the old mind tries to bring to its old body transforms that body into metaphor, adding a further level of meaning to biological processes. Aging deliteralizes biology just when we are most enslaved by it. Later years allow a second reading of what had seemed only literal biomedical problems. Other cultures speak of opening the "third eye," of consolidating the "subtle body." I understand this to mean that the psychological perspective takes first place, that one's primary ground of being has moved to the soul.

To deliteralize biology is not to deny biology. We cannot

deny any of the degenerative processes, any of the genetic influences. We are simply moving that furniture from foreground to background, moving our priorities. What may come first in time—bacteria, mitochondria, slime molds, chemical compounds, electrical charges—does not necessarily come first in value or thought. Moreover, "the gap between the most complex mixture of organic chemicals and the simplest cell has never been closed. Neither in theory nor in the laboratory has life ever been made from chemicals, no matter how complex they are," writes evolutionary biologist Lynn Margulis.[1]

Life may well depend on bacteria, molds, and chemical compounds, but thought achieves complexities that can't be reduced to prior building blocks. This is one of the great puzzles of thought: It can originate its own species, select unnatural ideas, and show its own evolution; and much thought that is quite unfit survives.

If old age is required for the fulfillment of character, then what about all those who never reach it, expiring before fifty? Maybe the common observation is right: "She died too early"; "His death was premature." By which we mean that their characters had not come to term. But what about the huge majority in other centuries, who lasted only into their thirties and forties? Were their characters unformed, neglected?

Perhaps older age was less necessary then. Old cultures (as do many indigenous ones still) ritualized the formation of character with initiations, festivals, and funerals; and elders gave collective instruction. Although their elders may have been younger in years than our seniors, they were still very much present, keeping an eye on each member of the group with a constant focus on character.

Ever since psychoanalysis reported on "fixated" and "arrested" character development and childhood "character disorders," even the idea of character became fixed to childhood. Psychology looked backward to study character development, neglecting the plain evidence that character reveals its full shaping force in most of us much later. We become characteristic of who we are simply by lasting. How we age, the patterns we regularly perform, and the style of our image show character at work. As character directs aging, aging reveals character.

———

Old age must have its gods, just as childhood and youth have their protectors, who inspire the exploits of first love and wild adventure. Later years invite other gods, whom it takes many slow years to know. Their claims and inspiration may be of another kind but they can no more be refused than the gods who call in youth. Discovery and promise do not belong solely to youth; age is not excluded from revelation.

We need to recognize how helplessly our thinking about the last of life has been trapped in disparaging ageism—a class concept that relegates all older people to a category with definite, inescapable handicaps owing to the breakdown of the organism and the exhaustion of its reserves. Biology and economics form our basic Western model. Ideas of soul, of individual character, and the influence of awareness on life processes have become accessory decorations to lighten the despair and disguise the "real truth" about old age.

The convention of ageism, this "real truth," makes us feel caught—and conflicted. Either we collapse into increasing pessimistic misery, already at fifty obsessed with the decay of mind and body, or we optimistically deny the "real truth" with a heroic program of spiritual growth and physical fitness.

The optimistic and pessimistic views share a premise: Old age is affliction. That is its "real truth." Whether you overcome it or succumb to it, the nature of old age is undeniably solitary, poor, nasty, and far too long. We can picture ourselves imprisoned in penury, set down in a bare nursing home, mad, mute, and smelly, waiting for the end.

Let us suppose that both optimists and pessimists are right, and right simultaneously. Yes, old age is affliction—especially, it is afflicted with the *idea* of affliction. As long as we regard each tremor, each little liver spot, each forgotten name as only a sign of decay, we are afflicting older age with our minds as much as our minds are afflicted by older age. The very repetition of our negative diagnosis of what's happening to us each time we see our face in the mirror shows how powerful is the idea to which we have harnessed our later life.

The mind likes ideas. It asks for fresh ones, even half-baked ones. It busies itself cogitating. The mind is naturally curious, inventive, transgressive. Older persons are advised to keep mentally active so as to delay the decline of brain function. Research says mind work builds brain cells. Use it or lose it—and it doesn't matter what you think about, as long as your mind is exercised like a muscle. But ideas are not merely vitamins that serve to keep the mind alert; the mind also serves ideas. By turning them over and taking them apart the mind keeps ideas alive and prevents them from stultifying.

Our ideas of older age need replacement. Like a hip that can no longer bear weight or a clouded lens that does not let you see out of your own head, we need to wheel our ideas into the operating room. But replacing outworn mental habits requires both attack and stamina.

To break with the usual ideas about later life, we may have to break through them. Then we may recognize that many conventional ideas that provide refuge from the oppression of aging are actually places to hide from the force of character.

It is comforting to believe that we are becoming wiser, that our judgment is more sober, that the alterations in our genital physiology are, as Sophocles said, a relief. It's easier to be old if we agree with ageism's clichés, and believe that attitudes coming to the fore as we age are not revelations of our essential nature but merely the effects of getting old. For instance, we are touched to tears by someone's kindness or we offer help to someone troubled. Instead of accepting gentleness as a trait of character, we pass it off: "I'm getting soft in my old age." Or, not my character but my age makes me utter those vicious racist remarks, give those miserly tips, spy on my neighbors. "I am only a helpless victim of aging": The tail, or tale, wags this poor little dog.

The longer we hang on to outworn ideas, the more they affect us negatively, acting as pathologies. The main pathology of later years is our idea of later years. It is your own youth and a culture whose ideas derive from youth that can make your old age morbid. After fifty or sixty another therapy begins—the therapy of ideas.

———

Aging has become the major fear of a generation. What we dread individually, society predicts demographically. Immense sums are spent to root out the causes of aging and hold off its approach. Yet old age advances with steady statistical progression. The coming years will more and more be dominated by older people. The twenty-first century may or may not be greened by ecological awareness, but it will certainly be grayed by its aging population. Developed nations are aging, rapidly; some are not even maintaining their birthrates as longevity increases. The perennial class struggle between haves and have-nots in the new century becomes one between Age and Youth.

Theodore Roszak's superb book *America the Wise* looks forward to the triumph of the old. Their sheer numbers could revolutionize society, moving it from predatory capitalism and environmental exploitation to what Roszak calls "the survival of the gentlest."[2] The increasing proportion of seniors in the population tips the balance in favor of values that, he believes, seniors hold dearest: alleviation of suffering, nonviolence, justice, nurturing, and maintaining "the health and beauty of the planet."[3]

Each of us can help further Roszak's vision: first, by exorcising the morbid idea of aging that keeps older citizens immobilized by depression, narrowed by anger, and alienated from their calling as elders; second, by restoring the idea of character, which strengthens faith in individual uniqueness as an instrumental force affecting what we bring to the planet.

An inquiry into character by means of aging takes us into unexplored terrain. The current maps of aging, which don't consider character, are factual and flat, leaving the reader with no peaks of inspiration, no depths of soul, while writings on character present themselves less as guidebooks to the quarries and springs of human nature than as handbooks for raising, and upbraiding, youth. Although moralists continually co-opt the idea for their agenda, the force of character is natural before it is moral. Character must first be investigated as an *idea* before we submit it to moral correction.

———

T. S. Eliot wrote that "Old men ought to be explorers"; I take this to mean: follow curiosity, inquire into important ideas, risk transgression.[4] According to the brilliant Spanish philosopher José Ortega y Gasset, "inquiry" is our nearest equivalent to the Greek *alethia,* an activity of mind that initiated all Western philosophizing: "an endeavor . . . to place us in contact with the naked reality . . . concealed behind the robes of falsehood."[5] Falsehood often wears the robes of commonly accepted truths, the common unconsciousness we share with one another. A therapy of ideas could free us from the conventions that keep our minds from committing interesting transgressions.

To see the force of character up close, we must become involved wholeheartedly in the events of aging. This takes both curiosity and courage. By "courage" I mean letting go of old ideas *and* letting go to odd ideas, shifting the significance of the events we fear. I mean the courage to be curious. Curiosity is one of the great drives of humankind, maybe of animal life in general; it's that desire to explore the world that sets the monkey and the mouse on their risky adventures. For us humans, adventure takes place more and more in the mind. This mental courage the great philosopher Alfred North Whitehead called the "adventure of ideas." "A thought," he said, "is a tremendous mode of excitement."[6]

A Preface from the Writer

Why do older people become moralists, sentimentalists, and radicals? They chain themselves to threatened trees; they march; they shout. They lecture Walkmaned ears about the moral decline of the West. We old ones are indignant, outraged, ashamed.

Why is fading away not enough; why can't we let our light go down behind the graying hills?

Sundown is the wrong image, for the sun's decline is marked with fire, a last protest, a call to beauty. We would enhance the day, not let it dim into the evening's serenity. "More light," said Goethe as his went out. Not sweet swallows twittering at dusk, but incessant vespers; summoning bells; a call to sermonize. "According to Plato, robbing the Gods and subversion of the state are excusable crimes when committed under the influence of extreme old age."[1] Is subversion what prompts this book?

Let's imagine we are pushed by our theme, Character, *and* the author's variation on that theme, *his* character, all the while carrying the moral, sentimental, and radical baggage that all old people have strapped on their backs. Writing as burden; writing as adventure; writing as disclosure.

I certainly do not want to read more words on how to build character and develop the wisdom of old age. C. G. Jung, despite identifying the archetype of the old wise man, and even identifying with it himself at times, wrote: "I console myself with the thought that only a fool expects wisdom."[2] "And the wisdom of age?" asks T. S. Eliot in *Four Quartets*.[3] "Had they deceived us / Or deceived themselves, the quiet-voiced elders, / Bequeathing us merely a receipt for deceit?"

Wisdom, compassion, understanding, and all the other qualities assigned to elders serve mainly as calming counterphobic idealizations against the bold force of the aging character, which lies coiled in an old soul, ready to spring. We old ones—halfway to the ghost status of ancestors and to the naked sensitivity of pure spirits—can flick a cobra's tongue once we get riled. The fuse is short. What I ask from a book is what I want to write: a book I'd like to read myself.

Writers in later years seem to have a narrow range of choices: memoirs of former life, revisions and retractions of former work, and defensive summations of former thought. Might there be another option?

Writing about the last of life cannot be an objective study, indifferent to the writer. His or her life is also on the line, so that the writing, if it comes from the heart at all, tells of the writer's character. Authors are characters in their own fictions. That a book announces itself as nonfiction and comes on as objective history, science, research, or truth does not cover up its fictive quality. You can't get rid of your character in anything you write.

An old soldier fights his first campaign again and again, in every new engagement. The last of life is filled with repetitions and returns to basic obsessions. My war—and I have yet to win a decisive battle—is with the modes of thought and conditioned feelings that prevail in psychology and therefore also in the way we think and feel about our being. Of these conditionings none are more tyrannical than the convictions that clamp the mind and heart into positivistic science (geneticism and computerism), economics (bottom-line capitalism), and single-minded faith (fundamentalism). The idea of character is alien to all three. I champion it precisely because it is so lost to the contemporary scene.

The idea will do some of the work for me, because ideas are

themselves forces that take hold of a mind, not letting go until we have given them some thought. The idea of character calls for writing; it wants to be written into print. The very word derives from *kharassein,* Greek for "engrave," "sketch," or "inscribe"; *kharakter,* which is both one who makes sharp incisive marks *and* the marks made, such as letters in a writing system. "Character" refers to the distinctive qualities of an individual, and can also mean a person in a work of fiction or played on the stage. The word wraps together the peculiarities of the author's individuality, the act of writing, and the book as a stage peopled by imagination.

But what kind of writing does an old person do, and how does one do it? "It is not always easy," said Wallace Stevens, "to tell the difference between thinking and looking out of the window."[4] How did Paul Valéry put it? "To think? . . . To think! It is to lose the thread." "Writing's the only thing that stops the thinking, you know," David Mamet told an interviewer.[5] And how does this writing that stops thinking proceed? Don DeLillo says, "The work . . . comes out of all the time a writer wastes. We stand around, look out the window, walk down the hall, come back to the page. . . ."[6] The tortoise determines the pace. We are borne on its back. Exploring as slow thinking, and thinking as slower writing: the old ones are connoisseurs of lost threads and downtime, because we can't keep up with usual thought.

Usual thinking about later years stops at death. That is not the destination of this book, nor is death a bold way to consider aging. What could be more usual than allegories of nature: splendid trees resting on solid trunks; an ancient turtle in the deepest seas; the full savor of aging wines and cheeses ("Ripeness is all")?

My passion cannot be satisfied with the evident, or even with the evidential. An end in death hardly takes us into forbidden territory. I think of Maurice Blanchot's exhortation "to write what is forbidden to read."[7] Everyone has an opinion on death. The subject invites easy clichés. As Woody Allen says, "death is

one of the few things that can be done as easily lying down."[8]
The rabbis, the monks, the ancient philosophers, the puer
preachers and channeling seers can fill your ears with teach-
ings. One empirical observation that seems to hold is that while
the gods may like those who die young, death prefers the very
old.

Death is not a subject for thought, because it cannot be sub-
jected to thought; death is beyond thought, unreachable by its
methods. Logic, demonstration, experiment—all come up with
blanks. Death has no psychology, no phenomenology other
than symbolisms, spiritualisms, and metaphysical speculations.
No one knows a thing about it. There is Nothing to think
about. "A free man thinks of death least of all things," said Spinoza.[9]

It is therefore crucial to our inquiry to *decouple death from
aging,* and instead restore the ancient link between older age and
the uniqueness of character. "Old" is present in degrees in
many phenomena whose character we admire, like old ships,
old shacks, old photographs; here, "old" refers neither to something grown into after middle age nor to something en route to
death.

To the question, "Why am I old?" the usual answer is, "Because I am becoming dead." But the facts show that I reveal
more character as I age, not more death. I am not denying my
eventual death, but I am not going to spend the last of life writing about what I cannot know.

Far more important is to look at older years as a state of
being, and "old" as an archetypal phenomenon with its own
myths and meanings. That's the bolder challenge: to find the
value in aging without borrowing that value from the metaphysics and theologies of death. Aging itself, a thing of its own,
freed from the corpse.

An eager interest in "old" as an archetypal possibility in all
things, as a given with human being as with all being, is what
our society misses, what older people miss particularly and
yearn to discover. For we know we must pass our days and

nights under the auspices of the implacable god who rules last years and wants sacrifice. The neglect of that god is reflected in the neglect of the aged, and in the old-age home with its routines in place of rituals, a secular sanctuary with no transcendent vision, no archetypal footing.

The restoration of the temple to the Old does not require a literal construction. It could begin as a literary one, a written construction by writing constructively. Let us be so bold as to imagine this inquiry as ritual, and may our thinking and writing invoke the powers that govern our subject. Let us imagine that a dedication is commencing.

A Preface to the Book

This book consists of three main parts, following the theme of character through three stages. These stages are not the usual three—childhood, maturity, and old age; rather, this book expands upon the changes character undergoes in later life. First, the desire to last as long as one can; then the changes in body and soul as the capacity to last leaves and character becomes more and more exposed and confirmed until a third piece of the puzzle emerges: what is left when you have left. *Lasting. Leaving. Left.* Three parts, three main ideas.

A book is built on ideas, this book especially. The capacity to entertain ideas and find pleasure in this entertainment has long been a justification for writing and reading books, and for holding on to them as valuable property. The section called "Longevity" examines what this idea more widely implies, what aspirations it carries, and how the idea of longevity can be extended beyond measures of biological efficiency and statistical expectations. Part One also examines the idea of "old," and why oldness is essential to what we love about the character of a person, a place, a thing.

Part Two looks into the physical symptoms that life brings as we begin to leave it, and searches those symptoms for their role in character formation. This is the heart of the book, because it goes to the heart of every life. "Leaving" attempts to show, in a dozen short sections, how the dysfunctions of aging convert to functions of character. The bothers, impediments, and dreaded symptoms of later years change in significance as we find their purpose. The idea to be entertained throughout "Leaving" as part of this book and leaving as part of life is that character learns wisdom from the body.

"Leaving" reconnects psychology with its first historical home, philosophy. The philosopher's task, said Nietzsche, is to "create values." Today, values are often discounted as mere personal opinions, and dogmatized or marketed to win converts or customers; thus, by finding lasting values in late life, the psychologist as philosopher will, as Nietzsche said, find "himself in contradiction to his today."[1] So this book is also a philosophical book. Old philosophers have been warmly welcomed in to have some say in creating values.

Between "Leaving" and "Left" I have set a brief Interlude, "The Force of the Face." This excursion claims that older faces are marked by character, that their beauty reveals character, and that their lasting power as images of intelligence, authority, tragedy, courage, and depth of soul is due to character. The absence of these qualities in contemporary society and in its public figures, this section claims, is due to the falsification of the older face on public view.

Part Three, "Left," wrestles with the ancient dictum "character is fate." For what is "left" is the piece of fate that each person's unique character embodies. To be unique is to be odd, different, atypical, unlike anything else anywhere; the oddities a person tries to whittle down to conformity during most of his or her life reemerge in late life to compose the image that is left.

Part Three points up the distinctions between the enigma of character and the abstract idea of self favored by psychologists, and also between character and the more popular idea of personality, appropriate to the charm of celebrities and the concerns of youth.

A further distinction runs through the whole book: between character as a moral structure inculcated by precepts and maintained by willpower and coercion on the one hand, and, on the other, character as the aesthetic style of lasting traits expressed in individualized tastes and behaviors. For what is left once you have left the stage is an idiosyncratic image, especially the one presented in later years, and not the moral precepts that you tried to uphold under the mistaken name of "character." One's remaining image, that unique way of being and doing, left in the minds of others, continues to act upon them—in anecdote, reminiscence, dream; as exemplar, mentoring voice, ancestor— a potent force working in those with lives left to live.

A preface should say what a book is about, a precis of the work as a whole. It will fail in this aim if the book is at all psychological. Why? Psychology is never *about* something, on the outside, a digest, an abstract. A book that invites the soul into its inquiry draws us inside its labyrinth. A preface tries to lay out the labyrinth on a flat map; it can't do justice, however, to the twists and turns and dark passages, or to the moments when clear light breaks through. Maybe the best this preface can do is to wish the book *bon voyage,* to acknowledge gratitude that the book exists and that it has found someone's hand and eye, even perhaps someone's mind and heart.

I

LASTING

Pour on; I will endure.

Shakespeare, King Lear

CHAPTER 1

Longevity

Moving, and being himself
Slow, and unquestioned,
And inordinately there, O stoic!

D. H. Lawrence,
"Tortoise Family Connections"

I n our competitive societies, "lasting" has come to mean out-lasting. "I've outlived my father and both grandfathers!" "According to my doctor, I should have been dead three years ago." "My insurance company is losing money on me. I've beat my pension plan and cashed in on Social Security, far more than I ever put in." Surely goodness and mercy shall follow me all the days of my life, because my life has outlasted the expectancy curve.

Not only have I defeated my genetic inheritance, my childhood schoolmates, and the actuaries, I've held off death itself. Life: a contest with all others and with death, so that living longer becomes a victory, repeating each year on my birthday that famous passage from St. Paul: "Death is swallowed up in victory. . . . O death, where is thy sting?"

Our experience of aging is so embedded in numbers of years left to live, as given by longevity tables, that we can hardly believe that for centuries late years were associated not with dying but with vitality and character. The old were not mainly thought of as limping toward death's door, but were regarded as stable depositories of customs and legends, guardians of local values, experts in skills and crafts, and valued voices in communal council. What mattered was force of character proven by length of years. Mortality was associated with youth: stillbirth and death in infancy; battle wounds, duels, robberies, executions, and piracy; the occupational hazards of farming, mining, fishing, and of childbirth; family feuds and jealous rages; epidemics and plagues that carried off populations in the prime of life. Cemeteries were dotted with the short graves of children.

The intimate coupling of longevity and mortality, that link which monogamously marries the archetype of old with the idea of death, takes hold of our minds only in the nineteenth century, with the advance of demographics. In France, positivist philosophy promoted the statistical study of populations, which moved death from the realm of the private and spiritual to that of sociology, politics, and medicine. The statistics on life span gave evidence of a falling death rate, which was read to indicate the progress of civilization. Society as a whole could prove its improvement by advancing longevity figures, and longevity could be advanced by new medical methods (vaccination, pasteurization, sterilization) and programs of public health (potable water; sewage treatment; ventilation).

Demographics took an even firmer grip when Emile Durkheim, one of the fathers of sociology, analyzed suicide statistics, showing that each district in France had a suicide rate that hardly varied from decade to decade. A predictable number of people in any given district could be expected to commit suicide in the coming year. When the incidence of suicide dissolves into the sociology of class, occupation, heredity, religion, age, and so on, then the act of suicide becomes a fact of sociology quite apart from the psychology of the individual who commits it. The statistical fact becomes a societal force, dooming a definite percentage in each district to die by their own hands. Data become destiny.

The life expectancy curve carries a force of its own. If you place yourself on it as a female teenager, say, you may have a life expectancy of at least seventy. At sixty, you find your expected longevity has risen; it may now be seventy-eight, or more. Once you arrive there, the statistical tables may place your life term at eighty-six. And so on. Even if you reach one hundred, actuarial statisticians speak of the "conditional probability" that there are a few more months or years ahead. Statistics confirm that the longer you last, the longer you will last, so that with each day of aging you may expect another day on the "actuarial curve to infinity." The curve cannot predict when your longevity will end; instead, it seems to bear you interminably forward. Rather than carrying you toward death and revealing the bare fact of your mortality, the curve functions as a statistical annunciation of immortality!

If "lasting" means more than outlasting statistical expectations, then what is it that lasts? What is the "it" that persists and endures? What could possibly last through all the events of a long life, remaining constant from start to finish? Neither our bodies nor our minds stay the same; they cannot avoid change. What does seem to hold true all along and to the end is an enduring psychological component that marks you as a being different from all others: your individual character. That same you.

———

But what does "same" mean? I have changed so much and am so different, and yet despite all changes something continues to assure me of being the same. I could lose my social identity, my physical configuration, and my personal history, yet something will remain the same, outlasting these radical vicissitudes. This book maintains that the idea of character provides this lasting core.

If sameness is the philosopher's term for what we experience as our character, we will have to discover more about this deep principle "sameness"—what it is and how it works. No small job, since philosophers have been thinking about sameness ever since Plato made the Same and the Different two of the most basic ideas to enter into the existence of things, form our thinking about them, and even make them possible.[1]

Philosophers play with the riddle of sameness. Take, for instance, your favorite pair of wool socks. You get a hole in a heel and darn it. Then you get a hole in the big toe—and you darn that, too. Soon the darned holes are more of the sock than the original wool. Eventually, the whole darned sock is made of different wool. Yet it's the same sock. In relation to its looks and in relation to its partner on your other foot, it is still the same sock. They go out together and lie together in the drawer; and even in relation to itself, its identity, it is the same sock, though it is different.

Here philosophers can apply Plato's archetypal ideas of Sameness and Difference. The sock is entirely different from the original as far as the wool goes, but its shape has remained the same. It never becomes a different sock, despite the radical material alteration. Its *material* is different; its *form* is the same.

By "form," philosophers mean the look of the sock, by which you recognize it as a sock. (Tube socks raise conceptual problems!) When can a sock not look like a sock and still be a sock? Philosophers also mean by "form" the sock's function as a match to its partner and to your foot (form following function). A third meaning interests us most: form as the active principle governing the way the new wool integrates into the old sock. Form is thus visible shape, and the shaping force of the visible. Do you see that we are getting closer to the notion of character?

A human body is like that sock, sloughing off its cells, changing its fluids, fermenting utterly fresh cultures of bacteria as others pass away. Your material stuff through time becomes altogether different, yet you remain the same you. Not one square inch of visible skin, not one palpable ounce of bone is the same, yet you are not someone different. There seems to be an innate image that does not forget your basic paradigm and that keeps you in character, true to yourself. The idea of DNA seems too tight to hold the psychic dimensions of our unique image. To embrace our complexity we need a larger idea.

Some Greek philosophers and thinkers of the medieval church attributed this consistency in the midst of alteration to the idea of form. Some further claimed that form individualizes. What causes each person and each thing to be different from other persons and things is the active force of form. No two forms can be alike. We are each maintained in our specific individual image by the principle of form. To use one of William James's suggestive terms, we are each an "each." As "each"es, we are unique because each of us has, or is, a specific character that stays the same.

It is most important here to grasp that we are unique *qualitatively*. You have your style, your history, a set of traits, and a destiny. You are essentially different from me by virtue of the lasting sameness of each of our individualized characters.

If the difference between you and all others were defined by physics, logic, politics, economics, and law, we would each be a numerical "one" without any necessary characteristics. The law says, "All are equal under the law"; politics says, "One person, one vote"; physics says, "No two bodies can occupy the same place at the same time"; economics puts all eaches into categories—consumers, workers, owners, employers. When each one is interchangeable with any other one, individuality requires nothing more than a different ID number. Since uniqueness depends on the qualitative differences forming the consistent sameness of your individuality, the idea of character is necessary to keep us different from one another, and the same as ourselves.

Let's go back to the sock. If what outlasts the wool is the form, then a preoccupation with physical decay—with where the sock is wearing thin—misses a crucial point. Sure, the sock is showing holes, and stitching up its weak places keeps it functional. But our minds might more profitably be thinking about the mystery of this formal principle that endures through material substitutions. Surely the lasting strength of character counts as much as the durability of wool.

Sometimes the stitchings and darnings don't take. Medicine watches carefully for rejection after transfusions, organ transplants, and bone grafts. The formal principle that guarantees sameness despite the introduction of exotic material is named by medicine the immune system. This system accepts or rejects replacements in accord with its own innate code. The new materials must be integrated into the integrity of the person. Or, as they might have said in church debates nine hundred years ago, the material must be accommodated to the form. It must fit my innate image. The new part—kidney, hip, or knee—must become *my* knee. The new wool must become *me*.

What converts this "it" into "me"?

—

Modern psychology, regardless of school, understands the assimilation of events into a "me" to be a function of character. The schools of psychology use other words for character, such as "personality," "ego," "self," "behavioral organization," "integrative structure," "identity," "temperament." These substitute terms fail to characterize the styles of assimilation that are the hallmarks of individuality. We each respond to the world differently, handling our lives in a particular style. The word "character" implies a bundle of traits and qualities, habits and patterns; it requires descriptive language such as we find in character references, letters of recommendation, primary school report cards, scripts and novels, performance criticism, obituaries. "Ego," "self," "identity" are bare abstractions, telling us nothing of the human being they supposedly inhabit and govern. At best, these words refer to the unifying sameness of people while neglecting their unique differences.

It is refreshing to discover that some of the oldest and most basic ideas of philosophy—Same and Different, Form and Matter—are actually at work in our daily lives, even in our bodies. I find it a delight that these old-fashioned woolly principles are immediately practical and can be discussed as bodily facts. Why must we be exhorted to build character and strengthen character when character is already a given, the staying power that keeps us who we are and holds our bodies to their form? Imagine the body as an ancient philosopher, the body as a place of wisdom—an idea already announced in the book titles of two medical specialists, Walter Cannon and Sherwin Nuland.

Cannon in the 1930s and Nuland in the 1990s both say the body's physiology knows what it is doing. There is a wisdom at work. The idea of character makes more understandable this governing wisdom. Moreover, if we regard character as more than a collection of traits or an accumulation of habits, virtues, and vices, but rather as an active force, then character may be the forming principle in the body's aging. Aging then becomes a revelation of the body's wisdom.

I am emphasizing form in the organization of matter for two reasons. First, to counter the hustlers of materialism, who ask us to buy the idea that we are complex pieces of biotechnology, best compared with the newest computer chips. Whatever form we show results from underlying biogenetic impulses. Form can be reduced to matter; it obeys matter's laws and is shaped by genetic material. Since matter does the forming, there is no need for a separate idea of form.

A succinct, well-written—and fantastic—passage from one of the world's leading cognitive scientists represents a host of similar statements in similar books.

> The mind is a system of organs of computation, designed by natural selection to solve the kinds of problems our ancestors faced in their foraging way of life. . . . The mind is what the brain does; specifically, the brain processes information, and thinking is a kind of computation. . . . The various problems for our ancestors were subtasks of one big problem for their genes, maximizing the number of copies that made it into the next generation.[2]

Why do I call this fantastic? Because this account of foraging ancestors, genes facing problems, and natural selection as deus ex machina leaves the big questions begging. Moreover, the statement is set down axiomatically, not as myth or as reductive simplification, but as self-evident truth, and that allows Pinker to go on blithely saying that psychology is engineering.

To reduce psychology to engineering brutalizes the meaning of form. My shape is more than how I'm put together. We all know that the way to last is to stay in shape, but "staying in shape" means more than working out. Do diet, exercise, and bed before midnight satisfy the needs of your shape? The first meaning of "shape" is "create," which relies upon a force that is invisible and yet makes each creature visible in its own style. The blanket term "information processing" covers over the history of subtle thought carried in the idea of form.

My second reason for insisting upon form is to keep a psychological viewpoint when addressing psychological questions. After all, life to the one who lives it is harassed by psychological perplexities for which biochemistry and brain physiology offer little comfort. Why live, why live long and with the probability of biological impairment are questions irrelevant to these sciences. Even should they remove the impairment and prolong the years, the "why" questions remain which no "how" answers can satisfy.

———

For old, hard, basic questions I like to turn to old, hard, basic thinkers, such as Aristotle—especially Aristotle, since he worked out the idea of form in relation to the body and the soul. This is what he says. The soul is the form of the body, "the original of its movement," and is the body's final aim or purpose. As the "substance of living beings," this form called *psyche* "influences" and "commands" the body, and is "more truly a part of the animal than is the body," although the interests of "body and soul are the same." The soul forms the body, yet it is itself without body and therefore it cannot be located in an organ, a cell, or a gene, any more than the form of the sock can be located in the wool. Because of the soul's incorporeality, "the soul's beauty is harder to see than beauty of the body."[3]

Millennia later, the Nobel Prize–winning physicist Richard Feynman also described the form that maintains sameness:

> The thing I call my individuality is only a pattern or dance. . . . The atoms come into my brain, dance a dance and then go out—there are always new atoms, but always doing the same dance, remembering what the dance was yesterday.[4]

To give more precision to Plato's form, Aristotle's soul, or Feynman's dance, tradition often uses the language of characteristics. The soul is concerned with goodness and beauty, with justice and courage, with friendship and loyalty. Character analysis and soul descriptions employ common terms such as "judicious," "sagacious," "knowing," "kindly," "timid," "ponderous," "vacillating." These qualities are the soul in action, patterning our movements and revealing the soul's formative power, which influences and even instigates our behavior. The soul is only an abstraction until we meet its courageous will to live or its judicious decision or its humor. The adjectives make our behavior deep or warm or timid or modest or gracious or cruel or prudent. They style the dance. We make soul by embodying and enacting adjectives that differentiate the soul's prolific potential. Through these characteristics, we come to know the nature of our soul and can assess the souls of others. Qualities are the ultimate infrastructure, giving purpose and shape to what happens to the body. They are the force in character. This leads me to think that living a long life serves soul-making by bringing to life the psyche's amazing collection of adjectives.

It helps to regard soul as an active intelligence, forming and plotting each person's fate. Translators use "plot" to render the ancient Greek word *mythos* in English. The plots that entangle our souls and draw forth our characters are the great myths. That is why we need a sense of myth and knowledge of different myths to gain insight into our epic struggles, our misalliances, and our tragedies. Myths show the imaginative structures inside our messes, and our human characters can locate themselves against the background of the characters of myth.

This structured, intentional, and intelligent idea of soul in general (and of each particular soul) as having definite character contrasts sharply with today's conventional clichés. What is said about the soul today is all gossamer, no fiber. "Soul" has become a refuge of mystery and mist, a fairytale land of fantasy and feeling, of dream and reverie, of mood, symbol, and vibrations, a passive loveliness, ungraspable and vulnerable as a butterfly's wing. The idea of form gives shape and character to soul and demands more rigor in thinking about it.

Form also gives a clue to the amazing energy of old people. According to Aristotle, the body is governed by its form, the psyche. The character of the psyche has no cause other than itself, and it fulfills itself by doing what it is naturally suited to do, which is also its pleasure. Aristotle calls this natural activity *enérgeia.* Energy is prior to and different from *kinesis* or movement and from *dynamis,* capacity or potential power. Your mental capacities and physical vitality may decline in old age, as might your mobility weaken, yet your character shows ever more energy as your form becomes more actualized.

Now, back to those socks. Curious that philosophers use socks for their lasting allegory, since "last" has a meaning deriving from the Old Norse *leistr* for foot and sock, as in the last of a shoe, that form of metal or wood used for building and repairing footwear. To stay in character is to stick to your last. In making a shoe, the last comes first.

One further sense of "last" bears on our longevity theme. This "last" refers to the tonnage carried by a ship, its capacity to hold weight; a last is a load, a burden.

These several meanings—lasting through time, lasting in the same form, lasting as bearing weight—together enrich the idea of longevity, extending it toward character. If "lasting" means remaining true to form, then what lasts is our character—and this can long outlive our life, because its influence and originating force are prior to the body's life and thus not altogether dependent upon it. Character lasts because it is the weight-bearing structure which we all too often feel as a burden. "I can't change; this is how I am, who I am." Building character increases longevity by making your image more indelible.

A caution: Although we last longest by staying true to form, that form may not be strong or straight or true. A structured character is not necessarily one laced together by moral virtues; its pattern may be facile, sneaky, even corrupt. But this, too, forms fate. Integrity does not mean having a granite jaw. A filigree is also a pattern; a house of cards is also a structure. The idea of integrity asks only that one be what one is and nothing more or other.

———

The Swiss tell a banker's joke. Father, owner of a small private bank, tells his two sons that one day he will begin to show signs of senility and his judgment will be impaired. He reminds them of the Russian proverb: "A fish begins to stink from the head." His sons must come to him then and frankly tell him that it's time to yield control. Years pass. Finally, the sons, always deferential to their father, go in to the old man and tell him what he had told them to say. The old man sunk behind a pile of papers, looks up with a zany smile and says: "Too late!"

A shadowy second meaning lurks behind the joke—as is often the case and as Freud delighted in showing. Not only does Father keep control even when he can no longer keep sane, but "Who shall run the bank?" represents the archetypal struggle between fathers and sons and dramatizes the role of longevity in that struggle. In some cultures, as long as the father is not dead, the son cannot come into his power. The Tallensi in Ghana say: "Your son is your rival." The inborn life force in each wishes to destroy the life force in the other.[5] Among herders in Somalia, "even when sons receive sufficient land and animals from their fathers to become independent household heads, they do not in fact operate as independent heads of households so long as the father is alive." It is a matter not merely of controlling resources and wealth, but of archetypal antagonism between spirits.

Older women also gain power by living long. "Ethnographic reporters from a variety of regions support assertions of an expanded role for women in late life." Not only do elderly women command the service of younger women, but in many societies they gain ascendancy in the village as a whole. In Melanesia, for instance, older women "are partly privy to men's cult secrets, which are rigidly kept from younger women."[6]

To hang on or let go—that is the question for the old. Medical terms allow us to recast the question as one of dosage. How much control should one cede at a time? Should one let go regularly, on schedule, in small diluted measures? Or massively, all at once, as in a purge? Timing is crucial. Lear's mistake may have been to let it go too soon, before all of him was ready. He did not know the royal roots of his own character; archetypal kingship could not be yielded so quickly. For the Swiss banker, it was too late.

The will to live long could be reduced to Nietzsche's will to power or to social Darwinism's misuse of Hobbes's "self-preservation is the first law of nature," a distortion that in turn reformulates into nasty selfishness Spinoza's philosophical definition of essence: "The endeavor to persist in its own being." The old don't give up easily.

Is that why mercy, justice, charity, and magnanimity are virtues preached to the aging? Who ever says to adolescents, "Be merciful and charitable"? They are taught how to get their due and hold on. "Pity," says Thomas Wolfe, "is a learned emotion. A child will have it least of all." The bywords for youth are "Achieve," "Look good," "Succeed," "Win." It is only us old ones who are asked to give away, reminded of Jesus' warnings that the rich have hard, if any, access to Heaven. (These warnings imply that the rich have only the other destination.) All such high-minded remonstrances may fail to affect an old person's greed, but they do serve to remind us of that greed, that tightfisted clutch which comes to many in later years.

So that it may not be "too late" to step aside, some societies practice geronticide. Of the ninety-five societies studied by research gerontologists Albert and Cattell, twenty killed old people.[7] Of the seventy-five that did not, only seventeen had legal sanctions in place. Some societies confront longevity violently, by beating, burying, strangling, or stabbing the elder who has become decrepit.

These killings are not incompatible with respect for elders; in fact, they often run parallel with supportive measures on old people's behalf. "Death hastening," as sociology has baptized these terminating procedures, has nothing to do with low or irregular food supply or with transmission of authority. Since mourning rites may begin while the person is still in the society, the killing is part of societal cohesion. The anthropologists observe that where there is strong group identity, geronticide is less likely. It is also less likely where there is unilateral descent—that is, where the elder merges with the ancestor. Some societies use the same term for "ancestor" and "grandfather" or "grandmother." And some use the same term for "dead" and for feeble, sick, decrepit.

What is decrepitude? In general, the word "decrepit" can be

applied to those who no longer fulfill their societal roles. Indigenous societies define it more socially than physiologically.
If an old woman can no longer milk a goat, tend a fire, or weave
a basket, then she is decrepit. To be blind, crippled, or wasted
may contribute to decrepitude, but physiology alone does not
define it, since this same woman, blind, crippled, and wasted
may still fulfill her role as, say, herbalist healer or storyteller. Or
she may embody a totem ancestor and carry a "power," so that
her mere presence is functional.

Modern progress lowers the value of older people at the
same time as it adds years to our lives. The longer we live the
less we are worth, and we will live longer! It is also commonly
believed that relatively traditional societies (Bangladesh, India,
Nigeria) pay more respect to elders than do relatively modern
ones (Chile, Argentina, Israel). Therefore, the importance of
old age is in inverse relation to progress. But this cliché does
not obtain in some very traditional, "archaic" societies where
geronticide is customary, nor does it obtain in modern societies
such as Ireland and Russia, where older people are held in high
regard.

Esteem for the old is less a function of modernization than
of the vitality of tradition that maintains links with another, invisible world, whether through religion, custom, superstition,
or folklore, or by means of common poetic speech. In both Ireland and Russia, poetry thrives.

The disparagement of values generally associated with the
old—tricks, skills, and know-how; familiarity with local lore,
songs and phrases, and superstitions; and just plain slowness—
lowers their value. In the context of these diminished values,
we more easily justify geronticide. We call this "putting them
out of their misery" and cover it over with more antiseptic
language such as "DNR" ("Do Not Resuscitate"), euthana-
sia, death-hastening, and assisted suicide. These practices take
place in private homes, nursing homes, and hospitals far more
often than reach the public eye. Even if our society does not
condone beating, stabbing, and strangling the aged, in some
hearts the wish is often there. Elder abuse has become a wide-

spread syndrome in the United States. Too often the wish becomes the deed. In general, in the United States, we hate aging and hate the old for embodying it.

It is not old age as such, but the abandonment of character that dooms later years to ugliness. We can't imagine aging's beauty because we look only through the eyes of physiology. As Aristotle said, "The soul's beauty is harder to see than beauty of the body." Without the idea of character, the old are merely lessened and worsened people and their longevity is society's burden. (Federal spending on those over sixty-five is five times greater than on those eighteen and under, of which much goes into juvenile detention, crime prevention, and jail rather than for their basic needs like food, learning, and shelter.) The idea of the disabled old prevents seeing the disadvantaged young. The old have become decrepit in our minds and in the societal sense of the word long before they are physically moribund.

Do we make the old "decrepit" by not clarifying traditional roles for them? Do they become dysfunctional because we have no functions for them? Productivity is too narrow a measure of usefulness, disability too cramping a notion of helplessness. An older woman may be helpful simply as a figure valued for her character. Like a stone at the bottom of a riverbed, she may do nothing but stay still and hold her ground, but the river has to take her into account and alter its flow because of her. An older man by sheer presence plays his part as a character in the drama of the family and the neighborhood. He has to be considered, and patterns adjusted simply because he is there. His character brings particular qualities to every scene, adds to their intricacy and depth by representing the past and the dead. When all the elderly are removed to retirement communities, the river flows more smoothly back home. No disruptive rocks. Less character, too.

Retirement also contributes to decrepitude, because the idea of retirement removes older people from useful social functioning. Retirement tends to congregate the retired into their own communities, isolating them from society at large and reinforcing single-issue political positions for their own protection and advantages. Of course individual older people find ways to be engaged, but the idea of retirement tends to foster a sense of entitlement rather than a sense of service.

Collected evidence shows that incapacitating decrepitude in the very old lasts only about three months. Even during these three months, two out of three of the "decrepit" have mental clarity, over half are seldom alone (receiving more visitors during this period than before), and half have only minor pain, others none.[8]

The last years, so valuable for reviewing life and making amends, for cosmological speculation and the confabulation of memories into stories, for sensory enjoyment of the world's images, and for connections with apparitions and ancestors— these values our culture has let wither. If you would find decrepitude and rectify it, then look to the culture and begin with the rigor mortis of its skeptical and analytical philosophies and the loneliness and dementia of its imagination.

If the value of a long life relies on a long résumé, we know that most of this past history is distorted or forgotten in later years, and not ready to hand for exercising judgment. We cannot come up with examples, cannot recall similar occasions. Only if their character has refined its intelligence, broadened its learning, and been tested in crisis can the old serve society. Society asks for qualities beyond stamina, remembrances, and piled-up "experience." That is why we turn to the character-revealing stories of aged rabbis, monks, and masters, and to interviews with old painters, writers, and poets. As witnesses to character they are larger than life.

"Resignation," defined in the dictionary as "uncomplaining endurance of adversity," often accompanies retirement and may be an early indicator of decrepitude. Before we resign from positions of control, we should ask ourselves what might come after. Sheer collapse into uncomplaining (or complaining) endurance? Perhaps *"re-signation"* needs to mean—rather than literal stepping down—resignification, rethinking the significance of one's position, re-visioning the idea of control so that it serves values that we have come to know are important.

—

Longevity enthusiasts neglect to mention that bad characters last, too. So do the helpless and the useless, the miserly who gather it in and store it away like fervent ferrets the longer they live. Sadistic cruelty may become ever more tyrannical as years eliminate other avenues of pleasure, and ambition does not necessarily moderate in later life. Simone de Beauvoir devotes vitriolic pages to the character of Marshal Pétain, the head of the French government that collaborated with the Nazi occupation. She shows him to have been mean, petty, selfish, vain, indifferent, harsh, evasive, obstinate, pretentious, prurient. None of these traits belonged to his old age as such; all of them belonged to his character, becoming more sharply visible in old age like a skeleton under the uniform and medals. Petain exemplifies character determining old age, not the reverse. This notion was well-known to classical observers.

Plato's most-read text, *The Republic,* begins with a conversation just to our point. Socrates says, "I enjoy talking with the very aged," and asks the old man Cephalus, "Is it a hard part of life to bear or what report have you to make of it?" Cephalus rambles a bit, but then focuses on the complaints of the old— "the doleful litany of all the miseries for which they blame old age." Then he concludes: "There is just one cause, Socrates— not old age, but the character of the man."[9] Cicero's *De Senectute* makes this same distinction: "Old men are morose, troubled, fretful and hard to please; . . . some of them are misers, too. However these are faults of character, not of age."[10]

If the qualities attributed to old age are independent of old age and rooted in character, then they may assert themselves at any time in life. A high school boy closed in his room may feel, as Cicero said, "ignored, despised and mocked at." And a thirtysomething woman, burdened with children, debts, and a self-centered husband, may become "morose, troubled, fretful and hard to please." The so-called psychology of old age can descend long before old age. Any day we may take to our beds and become querulous with friends, anxious about the future, and oppressed by the death we feel hovering. The autonomy of these assaults shows that their source is not in time but in something timeless, the archetypal forces affecting and directing character. In the classical tradition that lasted until very recently, myths personified these forces so that the condition described by Cicero, for instance, would immediately be recognized as having been brought on by Saturn, god of misers and misery.

The classical tradition did not look at old age through New Age glasses. Old age was not a cheery period, the last stage of growth. Instead, as the classicists saw it, longevity reinforces character, so what you got in old age was more of the same, much more. The English physician Sir Thomas Browne (1605–1682) also wrote a doleful litany:

> But age doth not rectify, but incurvate our natures, turning bad dispositions into worser habits and brings on incurable vices; for every day as we grow weaker in age we grow stronger in sin. . . . Every sin as it succeeds in time, so it proceeds in degrees of badness . . . like figures in Arithmetick, the last stands for more than all that went before it.[11]

Ambition may be one "incurable vice" that rarely weakens with age and, as Browne says, "grow[s] stronger." Scholars want to produce the definitive encyclopedic opus, architects their monument, CEOs the big merger—all force their later years into service for a lasting achievement. Sometimes there is ambition without any project or purpose save one's own self—a "senile ambition for everything," as De Gaulle (who knew a thing or two about ambition) said of Pétain.[12]

Many greatly successful old men (less so for accomplished women) lament that their importance was not sufficiently recognized. Gratitude gets a passing nod in moments of glory: The stars thank the team, the Oscar recipient effusively praises a memorized list of names. But as Greatness leaves the limelight, Gratitude limps behind, unable ever to quite catch up. Despite honors and awards, the voice of ambition still complains: "Never has anyone done so much, so well, for so many, and been appreciated by so few." Ambition still strives and soars.

Even after the last good-bye, ambition wants to affect what happens onstage, influence a successor, decide the division of the family goods, defeat one last rival (no matter who, even a brother). We cannot fully give up either the throne or the drive that took us to it.

About the renunciation of ambition T. S. Eliot writes these lines:

> Desiring this man's gift and that man's scope
> I no longer strive to strive towards such things
> (Why should the agèd eagle stretch its wings?)[13]

He reminds sentimentalists of the raptor inhabiting the aged, an unquenchable desire for yet more. Robert Bly writes in his poem "My Father at Eighty-Five":

> His eyes blue, alert,
> Disappointed . . . suspicious . . . He is a bird
> Waiting to be fed,—
> Mostly beak—an eagle
> Or a vulture . . . Some powerful engine of desire goes on
> Turning inside the body.[14]

We are beyond longevity here, and into the territory of character. To be the oldest senator ever, the last veteran of the brigade, the withered woman who never stops baking her pies for one day, even when she's in a wheelchair. No renunciation of desire here, because the desire masks itself as devotion, thereby making the days last and giving lasting significance to the days.

Since it is not age but character that is to blame for the intensification of peculiarities in later years, then the work of prolongation should focus on the main cause, the force of character, rather than on the "Arithmetick" of longevity. Merely pushing our minds and bodies through the hoops and rigors of prolongation misses the point. We should be asking: What preserves character? What helps it last?

We can answer by using the example of ambition. It lasts because it has an archetypal background. Its more-than-human demands present a myth in action taking a human being beyond itself.

Myths act out in human affairs, dramatizing our struggles and disordering our characters. Once we open the mind to myths, we can read mythology in life and not only in books. As Jung wrote, "The Gods have become diseases." The patterns of myth and their personified powers present archetypal styles of existence, which we cannot escape or be cured of.

In myth-based cultures, the gods are inhuman and eternal; *athanatoi,* "the immortals," the Greeks usually called their Gods. As forces in our characters, they make indelible those traits we cannot shed and cannot quite bring under our human control. A key to the mythical figure in the "disease" of ambition is the eagle.

Jupiter of the Romans, like Zeus of the Greeks, was often represented as an eagle, and under the standard of the eagle the Roman legions extended the ambit of the empire through most of the known world. Some of the Latin epithets for this greatest of all classical gods were *domitor, magnus* (great), *fecundus, altus* (high), *domitor mundi* (world conqueror), *omnipotens, summus, supremus, rector* (ruler, controller), *sator* (founder), *rex* (king).

When a Roman emperor was cremated, an eagle was released near the funeral pyre to conduct the imperial soul to the heavens. Only the eagle, it was said, could look directly into the face of the sun and be renewed by flying straight into the sun. The eagle's temperament was "exceedingly hot and dry," its appetite voracious. And it appears in holy contexts: John, the fourth of the Gospel writers and the most "spiritual," is represented traditionally by an eagle. It is the carrier of the highest spirit, of ambition's farthest reaches. One moment in the bright light and it is born again, ready to push ahead, with everything yet to come. (The eagle is the letter "A" in Egyptian hieroglyphics.)

According to the ancient lore of animals, the eagle dies because of the "increasing incurvature of its beak," which prevents it from taking food and eventually punctures its own throat. Bly recognizes this beak in his aged father, and Browne says that age "incurvates our natures." Nothing can bring the eagle down but its own aging. The lesson of the eagle teaches that getting old is the method mortality uses to cure the immortal sources of character, which push humans beyond their limits, "desiring this man's gift and that man's scope." Ambition finally eats itself up, becoming a torturing self-punishment; Prometheus, who wanted too much and went too far, was punished day after day after day by an eagle tearing at his gut.

A Greek vase painting depicts Hercules with Geras, the personified figure of old age whose name we still find in geriatrics and gerontology, the medicine and study of old age. Hercules, dressed in his lion skin, belted and girded, stands across from and towers over Geras, a bald, bent, emaciated figure with pendent and reversed (perverse?) genitals. He leans upon a thin, crooked stick, while Hercules holds a huge studded club. We see a classic confrontation of the archetypal hero with a woeful image of aging. The image parallels the many others of Hercules struggling hand-to-hand with Death (Thanatos) and with Hades, god of the underworld.

The ancestors of our culture show this confrontation in laments, in funeral inscriptions, in tragedies, and in graphic images. In today's world, the confrontation of heroic death-defying attitudes with the "problem" of aging has become interiorized, abstracted, and miniaturized. The archetypal allegory has become a subject of research, and the heroic opposition to aging takes place in laboratories and is encapsulated in jars of vitamins and supplements. The essence of the struggle, however, has not changed, because the struggle is mythical, as if an archetypal enmity exists between the muscled mind of progressive civilization, which slays monsters, drains swamps, and builds walls, and the little old man at the end of the road. Even if the weapons have shrunk to the smallest imaginable proportions, the rhetoric and strategy of the struggle are still those of battle, warfare, fight.

Today, molecular biology and nanotechnology—the manipulation of living matter at an infinitesimal level—lead the way. The first aim in longevity research has been to meet diseases with an ever more minute approach. Although Hercules' operations took place on a bulkier scale than defeating bacteria and viruses—he stunned a wild bull, strangled a lion, and cut off the serpentine heads of Hydra—the fantasy of destroying predators has not changed.

Overcoming disease is only the first aim. The next project is rejuvenation, the prolongation of life by reversing the process of aging itself. "What you need is a way of reversing aging, not just stopping it," says an editorial in *Life Extension* magazine, seducing its readers by expressing a popular wish: "You need a way to enable you to grow younger, healthier and more vigorous; a way to turn back the clock, so you can prance around in youthful splendor for *centuries,* not just *decades.*"[15]

The means to this ageless satyric prancing (laughable to the theatergoers of the ancient world) is nanotechnology, a field that calculates with ever smaller numbers, applying ever tinier instrumentation to the most minute bits of matter. Nanotechnology joins the realms of organic and inorganic, the models of biology and engineering.

Beyond defeating diseases such as tuberculosis and cancer, beyond even the slowing and reversing of aging, the ultimate Herculean project meets death head-on. We must extend or eliminate the conditioning categories that set limits to all life.

At a recent meeting of the senior associates of the Foresight Institute, the chairman did some "looking ahead":

> We as a society are confused about matter, space, time, and mind. Matter: people say we're running out of resources, but nanotechnology changes that. Space: people say we're running out of space, but space exploration removes that limit. Time: we're all supposed to be dying, but with nanotechnology we'll be able to keep youthful physiologies. Memory is mainly structure, and we can maintain it. Mind: with nanotechnology we can make machine intelligence systems a million times faster than our brains.[16]

The director of technology for the corporation Netscape also does some looking ahead:

> Many of the things people do are going to be unnecessary when matter can be rearranged arbitrarily. . . . [T]his gets into all kinds of bizarre stuff. Immortality. There's no fundamental reason why the breakdown of cell structures is inevitable. There's no reason death should happen. There's no reason decay shouldn't be totally repairable, there's no reason you shouldn't be able to design exactly the body you want.[17]

From what pattern would you design exactly the body you want? Barbie? Rambo? Hercules? What about bald, snub-nosed Socrates, huge Amy Lowell, "vertically challenged" Toulouse-Lautrec, John Keats who coughed out his tubercular lungs before he was twenty-six, Emily Brontë dead at thirty, or Sylvia Plath, whose tortures ended at thirty-one; or Franklin Roosevelt or Stephen Hawking; or sick Nietzsche, sick Schubert, sick Schumann, sick Chopin? So many have lasted admirably though deprived by their bodies of longevity.

Is there truly "no reason death should happen"? Is longevity mainly a problem for genetic engineering, to be tackled in the style of Hercules? However backward their technology, the Greeks at least knew the folly of desiring immortality, and they elaborated upon the complexity of this wish. They told tales of Tithonos, a human who was granted his wish of living forever, but who had neglected to specify at his present youthful age, so that he was cursed to live on and on, forever growing older.

More important than the cautionary horror stories about humans stupidly asking the gods for the wrong things is the fundamental necessity to the ancient world of human mortality. For, if humans can become immortal then we become equal with the gods—"deathless," as I've said, was the term chiefly used to describe them. Their essence is immortal; ours mortal. As they cannot die, we cannot not-die; the lines must be kept absolutely clear. Let's say we must die that they may be immortal. Our mortality assures them of their immortality; otherwise, there would be no absolute difference between humans and gods, and they might be nothing more than human fantasies, figures invented to fill up the heavens.

Hercules offers one more Greek lesson. Hercules does not age. Having overcome Geras/Hades/Thanatos, he can only go mad and lose his heroic strength, the very virtue that was the acorn of his character from the cradle. Antiquity provides no images of Hercules the older citizen, the counselor or mentor. Hercules knows nothing at all of aging. His view of it comes from his opposing stance to it. In his eyes it is bald, bent, and emaciated, "a tattered coat upon a stick" (while to Geras, Hercules must look like one of the studs in his club).

In our times, we must ask the Herculean sciences that would overcome Geras, whether by pumping iron and treadmill laboring or by minuscule manipulations of aging's genetic source: Does not the heroic approach contravene the mortal essence of being human?

—

The longer one lasts, the longer one wants to last—for the most part. You know the joke about the ninety-nine-year-old man, fighting off the day-care worker who is trying to freshen up his room: "Never mind the quality, I just want the quantity!" Just by adding another day, I again prove my worth. "Your mother's ninety-seven? How wonderful!" People smile, congratulate. No one says, "Ugh, that's tough; poor thing." Sheer numerical longevity, by becoming an end of its own, can keep at bay and in the shadow other meanings of "end," such as "finish" and "closure." Moreover, when the idea of lasting can be reduced to numbers of years and days, then medicine can justify its radical treatments to prolong what may no longer be wanted at all.

Of course there are virtues to longevity. For one thing, it's a favor to your descendants. It may lower their life insurance premiums and raise their life expectancy. You may yet meet your great-grandchildren and observe the repetitive twig formations of the family tree, or just watch one more World Series. Although statistics never lie, they don't tell the whole truth, either. They say nothing about *what* is being prolonged.

With aging, a curious kind of life extension happens without our doing anything to force it. After fifty we find ourselves at times more allied with our parents in thought, feeling, and memory than with our children. At seventy we seem more akin to a long-gone grandfather than to the very alive grandchildren who drop by from time to time like aliens from their spaceship. Our elders seem to be extending the soul by drawing it back to them. As interiority expands we move more easily into the small rooms of late-stage quarters, taking up less space in the world.

There is a clean distinction between statistical prolongation and psychological extension. The first doesn't speak at all to the worries about a possible afterlife, to growing scruples about clearing up and cleaning out, to added physical fragility and fear and already too-long-lived bitterness, shame, regret. That a life is lengthened says nothing about the character of those added days and years. They may have one quality only: length. Long nights and long days. While our statistics are improving, our soul declines into charts, schedules, and shots.

So it is not that longevity should be extended, if that extension merely adds more days of pain, sorrow, and incapacity. We need, rather, to extend the *idea* of extension. We need to broaden and deepen our thinking. Contrary to Matthew we might indeed add a cubit to our stature by giving more thought to extending the idea of longevity.

First of all, we can extend backward. Why do older people in our societies read biographies and turn on the History Channel? Why do they travel to the ancient sites of dead civilizations, visit museums, support historic preservation? What drives them to search for and restore rusted tools and outdated machines, buy old rootstocks for grafting, and repeat stencils, stitches, and quilting two hundred years old? Or catalogue old coins and spend their money on specimen rocks? Why do they fall for medicines touted as ancient cures, from amaranth to St. John's wort? Old soldiers become Civil War enactors; old women prefer historical novels played out in costumed settings. These are longevity fantasies of another kind than those offered by statistics.

The further back you can reach in imagination, the more extended you become. Your character and its oddities find echoes in similar characters who walk the streets of imagination, displaying essential qualities freed of the confusing disguises worn by actual family and friends. The soul is being replenished by the richness of images; even more, it is being absorbed into another imagination, which extends you beyond the confines of your actual condition. The old man in the trailer park lays out his buffalo nickels and Indian-head pennies, releasing fantasies that take him further afield than his game leg can. You can imagine living in a cold Scottish castle amid a fond family clan, awaiting Ulysses' return to Ithaca, mourning Lincoln's funeral cortège. You can discover the country, period, compatriots that suit your character and where your soul feels at home. Longevity becomes a kind of osmosis, merging with older lives in older places and older things. You are outliving your own life. No longer a lonely leaf on a drying branch, or even its fruit, you are sinking into the sapwood, and you become one hundred, one thousand years old, as old as the tree itself with the long life to come—a life of stories and scenes that go on and on, of shards and talismans that provoke ever-fresh fantasies.

Growing into the roots of tradition lengthens life backward. We can extend downward, too—into descendants; into apprentices who seek out our character traits—and also outward, into the family of images pasted into the photograph album and dumped in the keepsake drawer. I become extended through others whose images animate my solitary cogitations as well as through the daily others who come calling to see how I'm getting on.

Inquisitive curiosity into the lives of others extends our lives. This is not sharing; it is artful listening. The other person is a fount of lifeblood, which transfuses vitality into your soul if you can provoke the other with your listening. Probing— sniffing for lowlife, tidbits of scandal, tasty morsels of salacious gossip that awaken the appetite for the teeming life around you—loosens the limits of personal self-occupied concerns.

Backward, downward, outward extend a life beyond its borders and free it from attachment to personal identity, character freed of that greedy bully, Me.

The further back into history you can reach, the further down to what is later than you and lower than you, and the further out to what is not you, the more extended your life. Longevity is liberated from the time capsule. This is true longevity, an outlasting that is everlasting, for it has no stopping place.

CHAPTER 2

The Last Time

Last time I saw Chaplin, all he said was,
"Stay warm. Stay warm."

Groucho Marx in conversation with Woody Allen

L ast chance, last minute, last round, last inning, last exit, last ditch. Last rites, Last Supper, last days, Last Judgment. Last words, last breath. Last word, last laugh, last dance, last rose of summer, last good-bye. What an enormously weighty word! Why does it give such importance to the words it qualifies? And how does "last" bear on character? We shall have to find out.

Already I can tell you this: Our inquiry will aim deeper than the evident meaning of "the last time" as the end and therefore death. If that were all, the inquiry could stop here, satisfied with this banal result. Remember, we are eluding death all through this book, trying to prevent death from swallowing into its impenetrable darkness the light of intelligent inquiry. Death is a single stupefying generality that puts an end to our thinking about life. The idea of death robs inquiry of its passionate vitality and empties our efforts of their purpose by coming to one predestined conclusion, death. Why inquire if you already know the answer?

If a pair of socks helped us in the previous chapter, the fiction of a couple may help in this one.

"She just got into her car and drove off. That was the last

time I saw her." How casually the moment slips by, blurring into the everyday. But when the simple action is marked by "last," the event becomes an indelible image. "Last" makes an event eventful, elevates it beyond the everyday, leaves a lasting impression. Last words become "famous," last moments enigmatic emblems to ponder for years to come.

Why? Because what happens at the end of a sequence stamps its closure, gives it finality. Reverberations of fate. The events that composed the marriage, the love affair, the life together become essentialized into the last scene. She gets into her car and drives off. To her death in an accident? To another city and a new start? To another lover? Home to Mother? Back to her husband and children? Where she drives to belongs more to the next story than to the last scene of this fiction of a jointly attempted life.

Had she returned later as on any other day, the image of her getting into her car would have no significance and therefore would not last. But now it tells of character: the abiding character of the relationship—its commitment to casualness; its apparent openness, which conceals truth. Or it reveals her rebellious independence; or her adventurous courage; or her failure of nerve; or her diffident coldness. . . . It says something about his character, too—the unspoken feelings; the dulled sensitivity that cannot perceive and does not foresee. Their character together, his, hers—all compressed and expressed, at last, as she drives off.

So the last time is more than information for a detective's report. "Just the facts." She does, in fact, just get into her car and drive away. But the last time transforms the facts into an image. The impression of her at the curb as the ignition catches lasts because it is compressed into a significant image, a poetic moment. Other times are held captive by the last time and everlastingly signified.

Poetry depends on compression for its impact. The word for poet in German is *Dichter,* one who makes things *dicht* (thick, dense, compact). A poetic image compresses into a snapshot a particular moment characteristic of a larger whole, capturing its

depth, complexity, and importance. By putting closure to a series of events that otherwise could run on and on, the last time
is outside serial time, transcendent.

This kind of moment is hard to bear and hard to relinquish.
It feeds nostalgia, coming back to mind, a refrain that will not
let go. Older age makes room for what T. S. Eliot refers to as
"the evening with the photograph album," snapshots that bring
back a world.[1] Gerontology names these evenings "life review"
and claims that they are the main calling of later years. Since
anyone at any age can slip into nostalgic reverie, "later years"
can be taken less literally, to mean a poetic state of soul favored
by the old but not exclusive to them.

The last time turns love, pain, despair, and habit into poetry.
It puts a stop to, arrests forward motion, and lifts life out of itself. This is transcendence. We feel shaken to the bones, as if the
gods had stepped into the middle of our lives.

Transcendence of the daily does not occur until the epiphany
of the last time. She got into her car every day. The last time becomes utterly different. In no succession of events do we imagine any one moment to be the last. We can always come back
another time, do this again. "The last time" says there is no
"again." The last time is unique, singular, fateful. Pop lyrics
play on this poetic moment: "The days dwindle down to a precious few, September. . . ." (Maxwell Anderson); "The last time
we saw you . . ." (Leonard Cohen); "The last time I saw Paris"
(Oscar Hammerstein); "Last time I saw him" (Pamela Sawyer);
"This could be the last time . . ." (Jagger and Richards); "The
last time I saw George alive . . ." (Rod Stewart). "Again, this
couldn't happen again. . ."; etc. Each scene of life may be a last
time, like the morning she drove off in her car.

To call the last time unique, singular, and fateful makes it
sound inevitable and necessary, as if she drove off because it was
determined by her character. If character is fate, as Heraclitus
said, then this was her day to die. Or she had to cut out, because
"that's just the kind of freewheeling person she was; we should
have expected it." Yet it might have been a spontaneous impulse
to which her character gave in: "Enough is enough; I'm out of

here." A whim, seemingly out of character. We can't know. For us the story stops as the car pulls away.

Right here, we have to be careful. Character could become an iron law, permitting only those acts that are "in character." In that case, the idea of character engenders little waves of repression. "It's not my nature to do this, think that, want those, behave like this." Is there no room for the spontaneous, for moments of speaking, thinking, and feeling quite "out of character"? The answer depends on how we think about character.

I would claim that nothing is out of character. Character is inescapable; if anything were truly out of character, what would its source be? What stands behind a whim? Who pushes the urge and ignites an impulse? Whence do stray thoughts arise? Whims emerge from the same soul as choices and are as much part of your character as any habit. That last time belonged to her just as all the other times did. Belonged to her? Which "her"?

Her character must consist in *several* characters—"partial personalities," as psychology calls these figures who stir your impulses and enter your dreams, figures who would dare what you would not, who push and pull you off the beaten track, whose truth breaks through after a carafe of wine in a strange town. Character is characters; our nature is a plural complexity, a multiphasic polysemous weave, a bundle, a tangle, a sleeve. That's why we need a long old age: to ravel out the snarls and set things straight.

I like to imagine a person's psyche to be like a boardinghouse full of characters. The ones who show up regularly and who habitually follow the house rules may not have met other long-term residents who stay behind closed doors, or who only appear at night. An adequate theory of character must make room for character actors, for the stuntmen and animal handlers, for all the figures who play bit parts and produce unexpected acts. They often make the show fateful, or tragic, or farcically absurd.

Fitting them in is called by Jungian psychologists integration of the shadow personalities. Fitting them in, however, means first of all finding them fitting, suitable to your idea of your character. The Jungian ideal calls for a more integrated character, for the full boardinghouse with no exclusions. This may require conversion of the more disreputable and obstreperous to the morals of the majority, an integration leading to the integrity of the matured character.

These noble ideals are better in the recipe than on the table, for old people, as Yeats wrote and Pound demonstrated, are often disheveled, intemperate, whimsical, and closer to chaos than to the sober well-honed wisdom that the idea of integration suggests. The integrity of character is probably not so unitary; rather, the full company is onstage as at the end of the opera, when the chorus, the dancers, the leads, and the conductor take their uncoordinated bows. Life wants the whole ensemble, in flagrante delicto. Even the cover-ups belong to the character.

The study of how each of these characters belongs is a main activity of later years, when "life review" consumes more and more of our hours. Whether going through piles of papers and closets of things, or regaling grandchildren with stories, or attempting to write autobiography, obituary, and history, we try to compress life's meanders and accidents into a "character study." That's why we need so many later years and why, as the days shorten, more and more evenings are absorbed in the photograph album. Regardless of whether contrition, nostalgia, or vindictiveness marks our feeling as we turn the pages, we are as engrossed in study as if for a final exam.

We study our character and others' for revelation of essence, and we read actions such as her driving away as compressed expressions of this essence. She, at the curb, opening the car door, getting in and going off for the last time has become an indelible image, an objective shot corresponding to her character. We study this poetic particular for descriptive predicates that might lead to predictions about her behavior. Other images come to mind—other times when her eyes shone with a wild light while she sat behind the wheel; casual words of envy at a friend's freedom; her collection of lightweight, thin-soled shoes; a girlhood story of a dangerous hike. This cluster of images shows qualities that constitute her character: freedom, danger, movement, surprise. As these belong to her character, so they can be predicted. Her driving off should be no surprise— providing we compact her character into only these compatible images, arrange them into a coherent story, and omit all that does not fit in.

What does not fit in demands all the more scrutiny and a widening notion of character. All we need to do is stick with the image, allow its complications to puzzle us, and abandon such superficial ideas of character as habits, virtues, vices, ideals. Access to character comes through the study of images, not the examination of morals.

The daily world is notoriously poor in this kind of study. The little schoolboy killer was such a quiet nice kid; the serial murderer was hardly noticeable and seemed like anybody else; the baby-sitter who abused her charges was so prompt and tidy and polite. Our restricted notion of character restricts what we are able to see in people. If people are prompt and polite, nice and quiet; if they lack noticeable quirks, we expect them to be tidy in character. Unless we have a trained eye for the significant discrepancy, our predictions will invariably be wrong. The crime comes as a shocking surprise, an act altogether out of character. A culture blind to the complexities of character allows the psychopath his heyday of mayhem. No one noticed any oddity because no one had an eye for it. So after the horror he is sent to be "seen" by the psychologists who now, post facto, know what to look for and will, of course, find it.

We are as we appear, yes, but only when appearances are read imaginatively, only when the perceiving eye studies what it sees as a lasting image. This eye looks at the facts for the significant gesture, the characteristic style, the verbal phrasings and rhythms. This eye is trained by the visibilities of human nature. It learns from "people-watching," from movie close-ups, dance postures and dinner parties, body language, and the street. It sees an image, which Ezra Pound defined as "that which presents an intellectual and emotional complex in an instant of time."[2] Especially, I would add, in that instant we see as "the last time." The older we get the longer we look, and want to look.

A woman of one hundred and three, living in Nevada, described her desire:

> I want to start a wedding chapel. . . . I would just sit in a nice chair and let . . . whoever I hire do the strenuous work. The reason I'd like a wedding chapel is that I could study the people. I could see what kind of man she's going to marry, and what kind of woman or girl she is. I can tell, I can tell.

Al Hirschfeld, artist and caricaturist, at ninety-five declares:

> What's a man to do? Sit around some sun-soaked beach all day? Watching the waves? Or playing golf?. . . Human beings fascinate me. People. I used to love just sitting in the window of the Howard Johnson's at Forty-sixth and Broadway, drawing the constant parade of people passing by. . . . I'll draw a bow tie, or a cane, or jot down one word or make a sketch that brings back an entire scene.[3]

The eye for the image cuts to the essential.

In our overpsychologized culture, psychological testing substitutes for this seasoned eye and prevents its development. Instead of looking, we test; instead of imaginative insight, we read write-ups; instead of interviews, inventories; instead of stories, scores. Psychology assumes it can get at character by probing motivations, reaction responses, choices, and projections. It uses concepts and numbers to assess the soul, rather than relying on the anomalous eye of a practiced observer.

The anomalous eye is the old eye. The older soul, aged into its own peculiarity, cannot, in fact, see straight at all; it favors the odd. Love of the odd may appear early in life, with the affectionate nicknames children give one another and that single out a particular feature or trait of character. But usually youth prefers conformity, trying to adjust or smother what does not fit in. In late life, having now become studies in uniqueness, we look for companions as odd in their ways as we are in ours. Similarities in daily routines, similar past experiences, parallel symptoms, common backgrounds are not comforting enough. The fun, the love comes with companions in uniqueness. The odd couple: a couple of oddball characters.

The term "gerontology" should more rightly refer to the kind of study we do with our old eye than to the study of old age by young psychologists. Our studying does not aim to uncover why she got in the car and drove off. The cause is already given: It was necessary because it was in her character. No use laying out the reason—she felt trapped; she had a secret; it was her time; she went schizoid and fled from love, or was a paranoid and fled from demons, or a sociopath and took the money and ran. We have little interest in exculpatory causes, such as her mother, her childhood, her horoscope, her awakened feminism. Conventional generalities explain nothing to the old observer. The anomalous eye just likes to watch, to sink deeper into the puzzle of human character which increases tolerance for human oddity.

Instead of coming up with reasons and diagnoses, we study the image. Our curiosity focuses upon the image of the last time, on her behavior as a phenomenon, on the image as an epiphany, for it is the image that lasts and can be reflected again and again in a variety of stories, exhibiting character in action. She was performing a drama, in which, as Aristotle said, character is revealed through action.

Her last scene is also dreamlike, a tableau: the curb, the car, the key in the switch. In a dream we never know the motive for anyone's action or the diagnosis of anyone's problem. Psychology begins in the morning. We do not know the reasons for what dream people do, how they were treated in childhood, or even why they are there at all. The more the dream strikes us as an image—and each dream is a one-and-only, last-time dream—the less we can formulate it, yet the more we can return to it and draw from it. Everything we look upon seems odd, as if seen for the first time, or the last. Something redemptive happens. "We are blest by everything, / Everything we look upon is blest," writes Yeats—the last, and lasting, lines of one of his reflective poems on aging published when he was sixty-eight.[4]

Blessing is the one gift we want from the old, and the one great gift only they can bestow. Anyone can applaud above-average achievements and award the outstanding. The old, however, are able to recognize the beauty that is hidden from usual sight, not because they have seen so much through the years, but because the years have forced them to see so oddly. What one needs blessed are the oddities of character specific to our solitary uniqueness and therefore so hard to bear. I can bless my own virtues, but I need a well-trained, long-suffering eye to bless the virtues concealed in my vices.

A culture is preserved by the old. This cliché usually means that they guard the old ways, the old knowledge, the old stories; they are wise and give prudent counsel. Rather, I think, culture is preserved by the old because they enjoy the odd, study others for it, and locate the essence of character in what is peculiar to each phenomenon. A culture that does not appreciate the character of anything eccentric to its model tends to homogenize and to standardize its definition of the good citizen. The old preserve culture by means of the stubborn sameness of their unsuitable peculiarities.

The increasing importance of oddity as we age shifts the idea of character from the constitutive center of a human being out to the edges. The character truest to itself becomes eccentric rather than immovably centered, as Emerson defined the noble character of the hero. At the edge, the certainty of borders gives way. We are more subject to invasion, less able to mobilize defenses, less sure of who we really are, even as we may be perceived by others as a person of character. This dislocation of self from center to indefinite edge merges us more with the world, so that we can feel "blest by everything."

C. G. Jung spent his more than eighty years following the Delphic maxim "Know thyself." Self-examination and inquiry into the self of others was his lifework and formed his theory. Yet, amazingly, this is what he writes on the very last page of his autobiographical memoir:

> I am astonished, disappointed, pleased with myself. I am distressed, depressed, rapturous. I am all these things at once, and

cannot add up the sum. I am incapable of determining ultimate worth or worthlessness; I have no judgment about myself and my life. There is nothing I am quite sure about. . . .

When Lao-tzu says: "All are clear, I alone am clouded," he
is expressing what I now feel in advanced old age. . . . Yet there
is so much that fills me: plants, animals, clouds, day and night,
and the eternal in man. The more uncertain I have felt about
myself, the more there has grown up in me a feeling of kinship
with all things. In fact it seems to me as if that alienation which
so long separated me from the world has become transferred
into my own inner world, and has revealed to me an unexpected unfamiliarity with myself.[5]

Let us review for the last time her departure. That image
offers one more allegory for imagining character. Her move
exposed a dimension that he at the door had never been able to
perceive, owing to the assumptions he made about her character. What he could not see before, he sees only too clearly now,
in his imagination. Perhaps, until she turned the key, she, too,
was ignorant of this depth of potential, this eccentricity. Nor
had either of them a foreboding of sudden death—if that is
where she went.

We come to realize that character dissolves into stories about
character. We become characters in these fictions; this implies
that the very idea of character also becomes a fiction—and
therefore vastly important, for it generates imagination much
as her image in this chapter provoked our imagination to invent
fictions about her character and about the idea of character.

This is why the idea of character is so needed in a culture: It
nourishes imagination. Without the idea we have no perplex-
ing, comprehensive, and long-lasting framework to ponder; instead we have mere collections of people whose quirks have no
depth, whose images have no resonance, and who are distinguishable only in terms of collective categories: occupation,
age, gender, religion, nationality, income, IQ, diagnosis. The
sum of these adds up to a faceless Nobody, not a qualified Each.
Without the idea of character, no single person has a lasting

value. If each is replaceable, each is also disposable. The social order becomes like a battalion under fire; we are all replacements, filler for empty slots.

Character itself dissolves into fiction, as she does in our imaginings about her character, but the *idea* of character makes the fiction lasting. The idea keeps us inquiring, makes us look more closely at the snapshots. Her image spurs our imaginations. We want to know her better, see who she really is. Yet "who she really is," her literal character, is only literary, only a figure in the stories in which she is the main character, and that is what lasts even when she has gone.

We, too, last as fictional images, whether in the reminiscences of family, the gossip of detractors, or the reports of obituarists. Our character becomes the fertile source of fictions that add another dimension of life to our lives even as we fade as actualities. Jung realized this truth in his very late years, finding that he had become unfamiliar with the character he had assumed himself to be. His self-same reality became porous, indefinite, susceptible. As he wholly loosens into the world of "plants, animals, clouds" and is assimilated by the natural world, his character in the imagination of the human world continues to last, and goes on generating stories of who he really was.

Old

> . . . what terrifying teachers we are for that part of creation
> which loves its eternally childish state.
>
> *Rainer Maria Rilke,*
> Sonnets to Orpheus 11:14

I want now to study the idea of "old" all on its own, independent of aging. **Distinction between Aging and Old**
should be printed in bold letters—as would have been the case
in the old and ageless books of other centuries—for the difference is as important as the one between aging and death, discussed in the first preface. When we muddle these three terms,
we miss the importance of each. For "old" is a category unto itself, not necessarily implying either the process of aging or the
approach of death.

When we begin to inquire into old—old cut free from the
downward drag of aging and the fearsome bogey of death—we
find right off that what we value most about things called old is
precisely their deathless and ageless character. Old masters'
paintings, old manuscripts, old gardens, old walls do not bring
to mind dying but everlastingness. Paleontology, archae-
ology, geology—studies of the old. We visit Old Towns, preserve old sites, collect old silver, glass, cars, instruments, toys.
These old things and places seem more potent guarantors of
a tomorrow than do the young bodies of marines and adolescent girls—who, for all their hope and bloom, seem more
susceptible to fast fading and death than the bent old woman

marching to her bus stop and the veterans wheeling around the hospital.

Old is a visible condition, independent of years. There are old children with old eyes, whose oldness displays their distinctive character, not that they are near to dying; old souls, who seem to be waiting for time to catch up so they can finally come into their own. Estranged in childhood, distressed in youth, they have been old from the beginning. In fact, "old" and "soul" cannot do without each other. There are old words so packed with connotations that they grow more significant instead of aging into obsolescence. There are old texts, like those of Homer and Ovid, Heraclitus and Sophocles, that require new translations every generation: The translations age, but never the texts.

What about the old things you live with? Are they aging, dying? The old chair the cat prefers; the old tumbler your hand enjoys holding for your evening whisky. "I love this knife; I couldn't do without it." We say "love" more often about things—tools, shoes, hats—than about persons. Old is one of the deepest sources of pleasure humans know. Part of the misery of disasters like floods and fires is the irrecoverable loss of the old, just as one of the causes of suburban subdivision depression—and aging and death—is the similar loss of the old, exchanged for a brand-new house and yard. Old things afford a supporting vitality; without them, we find it harder to be alive. Moved from the old place to the new, deprived of their old things, old people more easily let go. What is old has slowed their aging and postponed their death. We need the old pleasure-giving things, which reciprocate our love with their handiness and undemanding compatibility.

"Old" is itself a very old word, supposedly deriving from an Indo-European root that means "to nourish." Tracing the word into Gothic, Old Norse, and Old English, we find that something "old" is fully nourished, grown up, matured. Today, when we inquire into someone's age, even if that someone is a small child, we ask, "How old is she?" and are told, "She is four years old." At whatever age we are we identify ourselves with a specific quantity of oldness, having and being "old."

Old English manuscripts love *eald* (old); it is one of the fifty most frequently appearing words in the medieval corpus of legal, medical, religious, and literary texts and occasional scribbles. And it mainly carries a positive meaning. Of forty-nine compound words that incorporate *eald,* only eight are clearly negative, like "old devil." To include *eald* in a compound generally brings benefits: trustworthiness, venerability, proverbiality, value.

A goodly portion of the English language descends from the eighth-century epic poem *Beowulf,* which, some scholars contend, places oldness among such virtues as nobility, mercy, esteem, and power.[1] With the daring adventure and revolutionary thought of the Renaissance, however, "old" begins its decline. Shakespeare used "old" as an instrument of insult and ridicule and he frequently disparaged the word by coupling it with unpleasant partners: "old and foul," "old and wicked," "old and miserable," "old and deformed." "Reading modern idioms using *old,*" writes the medievalist scholar Ashley Crandell Amos, "is a lowering experience, and a drastic contrast to the old English patterns."[2] Since "words do not live in dictionaries; they live in the mind," as Virginia Woolf put it, the old mind is lowered by the lowering of "old" to its present undesirable condition: old maid, old-fashioned, old guard, old boys, old witch, old fogey, old fart.[3]

Some of this contempt comes from a superficial habit of mind that can grasp meanings only with the tool of contrasts. "Old" then suffers from clichéd comparisons with "new," "fresh," "young," and "of the future"; its meaning narrows to the stale, the worn, the dying, and the past. When "old" gains its definition only by pairing, it loses its value. In a culture that has identified with "new" ever since Columbus, "old" gets the short end of the comparative stick, and it becomes ever more difficult to imagine oldness as a phenomenon apart from the lazy simplicities of conventional wisdom. To escape from the negativity of "old," don't leap for the new, which reviles the old as its opposite. Don't fall for thinking in opposites. That mistake continues to curse the New World of the American continents with its basic syndrome: addiction to newness and futurism, which makes anything "old" retro, passé—"a bucket of ashes," as America's American poet, Carl Sandburg, wrote. To escape the spell that the new casts on the old, dive into the old every which way you can: old ideas, old meanings, old faces, old things.

Oldness is an adventure. Stepping from the bathtub, hurrying to the phone, or just going down the stairs presents as much risk as traveling camelback in the Gobi. Once we were down the stairs and out the door way ahead of our feet. Now who knows when the trick knee will give out or the foot miss the tread. Once we learned from the fox and the hawk; now the walrus, the tortoise, and the moose in a dark bog are our mentors. The adventure of slowness.

—

The appreciation of any phenomenon calls for a phenomenological method. To know your mother, study *her,* don't compare her with your father, or her sister, or the mother of someone else. Our approach tries to penetrate the phenomenon itself. We walk around it from many sides (circumambulation), expand it by turning up its volume (amplification), distinguish among its everyday appearances (differentiation). We want more of its character to shine forth; epiphanies, revelations. To inquire into oldness by thinking also about youth and freshness and the future diverts the inquiry into a study of opposites, rather than bringing us closer to the nature of oldness—that quality we feel in old things and places, meeting old friends, going to old movies, watching a pair of old hands at work.

The world nourishes when we feel its oldness. The human soul cannot draw very much from the New World of discoveries or from futurism's Brave New World, which makes nothing that lasts and whose swiftly obsolescent generations are far shorter than those humans enjoy. Not those worlds, but this old, old world; the very word "world" was once spelled *wereald, weorold:* this nourishing place, so full of *eald.*

It is as if "old" were hidden inside "world" much as the

Gnostics' Sophia and the Kabbalists' Shekhinah were the soul concealed within the created world. Sophia and Shekhinah are figures of ageless wisdom, the intelligence of soul abiding in all things. As the soul of the world is an old soul, we cannot understand soul without a sense of old, or old without a sense of soul.

What is it but the character of old words, things, and places that brings comfort to our daily lives? They show more and more character. That whisky tumbler has character partly because it is brimming with connections flowing in from a multitude of memories. Like Proust's cookie, the glass is rich with other occasions, a talisman of recall, the objective correlative of emotions and thoughts. It is the "same old" tumbler, old because it is the same one and same because it is the old one. I have held it in my hand and it has hand-held me, settling me down, getting me through—and I take good care of it: reciprocity. I find myself with it and come back to myself through it. It is what I live with, and most closely, granting me the feeling in its presence of something truly "mine." It is an external soul, like those ensouled objects of indigenous people without which they become lost, sick, or crazy. In any other glass, the whisky would merely be a drink.

Even when chipped, blunted, and threadbare from overuse, old things have acquired character—from familiarity, from utility, and sometimes from the beauty of luster, patina, or design. Or simply from being old, the being of oldness. Without this sense of old as a state of being beyond beauty and utility, we cannot come easily into older years. Instead of the lasting that oldness signifies, the richness of accumulations coupled with the shedding of inessentials, we moderns take old only as the result of destructive time, as a last stage linked to death rather than to lastingness.

Old brings out character, gives character, and often substitutes for character in our common feelings. "That old house" means a house with a strong character, and "my old dog" refers to her character traits that are evident and familiar. I do not call the house old simply because it was built in 1851, or the dog because of her sixteen years. Numbers are impartial, applicable without feeling, and therefore are so useful for the uninvolved stance, whereas the adjective "old" bears emotions, and so I say "old" for things deeply loved and just as deeply reviled. The best I can say of someone, and the worst, is that he is old.

My granddaughter picks up a plate and I say, "Take care; that belonged to my grandmother, your great-great-grand-mother!" I am telling her that the plate is dear, rare, valuable, vulnerable. I am asking her to accommodate her young hands to its oldness. She has to adjust to its pace, handle it gently, walk it slowly across the room, feel its fragility. I am telling her that it has lasted and that it is valuable because it has lasted, proving its sturdy reliability and also its frailty. History has layered the plate with years of time, but it is not time alone that gives the feeling; it is the oldness as character, character as lay-ering, a complexity that makes the plate unique and calls from us respect.

Aging opens the door to "old," and old age opens it yet wider. That could be its point. Can we know the world's oldness or enter into the character of anything until we are ourselves old? That the old are burdened with wisdom means that they know the ways of the world because they are old, as it is. They share the same state of being.

Wearing thin and wearing out, of course, but old also holds time affectionately. It loves years, decades, centuries. Old holds off change, bringing all old things nearer to permanence.

Time is not only destructive; it toughens as well as weakens. Time lasts; it keeps on going and going and going and therefore is no enemy of age or of old. But time is indeed destructive to youth, which it eats away and finally stops dead. So when we hear of the corruption caused by time, we are listening to youth speaking, not age.

The desert monks of early pious Christianity kept youth at a distance, warning of its danger to the older person's purpose. Youth brought in the demonic. The monks' warnings focused not merely on youthful unruly behavior, sexual attraction, and lack of studious knowledge. The pedophobia of the older monks acknowledged that the perspectives of youth were poison to the tasks of constructing their character, which required silence, compunction, self-control, endurance, vigilance, patience, and discretion.[4]

The habits of the early English language seldom put youth and age together in the same phrase. Today, we compliment the elderly on their youthfulness, bringing the two archetypal kinds of existence in closest proximity and letting the empire of young colonize the old. But in Old English, the old and the new will rarely be found side by side. A hard line between the two must be kept: "Don't try to judge the old and the young, the sick and the healthy, the rich and the poor, or the learned and the lewd by the same rules," advises a psychology text of the time.[5] To realize that old is like a species of its own, study an aged elephant or horse, your house cat or dog. See it for itself, as if the young of the species were of another breed.

What does an old monk have to say to an old person today? To stand as we are in our character as older people we need to keep youthful attitudes at arm's length. Maybe young people, too—not because their fresh bodies and vacant minds lure us toward them, but because we expend into their lives too much of our spiritual substance. If "old men ought to be explorers" because "here and there does not matter," as T. S. Eliot said, that exploration is of oldness itself, mapping that terrain and entering that kingdom.[6]

We have a huge business to tend to, and with little profit. Reviewing our life for its character costs more than passing out free advice to young people as their supposed mentors. Mentors and elders are recognized for their character; they have character, are characters. Otherwise they are simply oldsters, a term that is derived from "youngsters" and that collapses old and young into a sterile hybrid of cheerful consumerism.

The plight of youth in contemporary culture energizes our compassion. The destitution of children and the exploitation of adolescents call us to step in and take part, for we are not ancient desert monks but living citizens. But what is our part? It is to incorporate oldness rather than to go along with a hypocritical culture that extols youthfulness while neglecting, trivializing, manipulating, and even imprisoning actual young people. We play the part the old have always played: preserving and transmitting knowledge and modeling on the ramparts of actual life the force of character.

Only if it's right to stick to our own last can I make sense of the terrifying, spontaneous pedophobia rising up in me at the noise of boys, their chase of fun and sleep and brand-new stuff; at a gaggle of girls, their breathy intonations and sullen reluctance; at the ignorance of youth that comes on as innocence; at the clothing, the manners, the music. I can so quickly become a crank, cruel, mean, and hateful, ruining every direct engagement with young people. If the task of old people is to enter civilization in young people's behalf, why does the old soul harbor this pocket of hatred? Must it not be purged?

I think blessed, instead. As with any symptom, we need to see its possible purpose. Pedophobia leaps up like an instinctual reaction. It functions protectively, keeping youth away. The monks say youth tempts the old from our principal occupations: character and our aging fate. Rather than blurring the distinctions between old and young, and confusing their different tasks, the sudden hatred says that companionship with youth, except in rare cases, cannot be our calling and leveling cannot be our mode; sharing is altogether illusory. Attending upon the character development of the young, important though it may be, is less our daily job than uncovering our own. To be fully old, authentic in our being and available in our presence with its *gravitas* and eccentricity, indirectly affects the public good and thereby their good. This makes oldness a full-time job from which we may not retire.

This word or idea "old" that we old ones enact is more than a word and an idea. It is an image of compacted layers. The mind's eye can imagine old in the elephant, gnarled trees, Great-Aunt Evelyn wrapped in a blanket, the neighborhood alley before it was redeveloped. Images spring to mind. That is why "old" is the appropriate term for people in late life. They are called "old" not simply because of their aging, but because of their value as images of oldness.

On the one hand, life review is the study of one's personal biography and its main character who lived it, tells it as a story, and now reviews it as critic, appraiser, judge, inquisitor, and defendant. Life review is an activity that separates the strands of "old"—the aged sensibility, the olden times, the tottering body, the accumulated richness of days, the whitened head of the authoritative elder, the forgetful fumbling foolishness that lapses into fantasy. These strands of complexity give "old" its substance and present themselves together "in an instant of time," fulfilling Pound's definition of "image." Old age means arrival at the condition of an image, that unique image that is your character.

Far better than comparing "old" with external ideas like "fresh" and "young" would be teasing apart the web of ideas stuffed into that one short syllable. The Bible needs at least nine different Hebrew terms plus many variations, while our English language compacts them all together.

Olam = ancient olden times. *Gedem* = days of old, as before time. *Rachoq* = old as far away and long ago. For old people like Sarah and Job and for old counselors there is *zaqen*. *Ziqnah* = old age. "Cast me not off in the time of old age; / When my strength faileth"—a theme restored in our time and reduced to personal love in the Beatles' line: "Will you still need me, will you still feed me, when I'm sixty-four."

There is *sebah,* a good old age of gray hairs, full of days; *balah,* a sad one, worn out like old clothes. Then there is *athaq,* to be removed (advanced in years): "Wherefore do the wicked live, / Become old, yea, wax mighty in power?" Also, *y'shiysh,* to become very old, and *yashan,* which is said of old things like stored fruits, gates, pools.[7]

These kinds of old, and more, course through us. These are the strands and rhythms of human complexity. One morning we feel we are a bag of bones, a tattered coat upon a stick; on another day, we belong to a time before time began, an anachronism as old as Methuselah. Some days we know ourselves as a number only: 76, 81, 91.

I am a forgotten castaway, a sharp-eyed wise man, still standing like an old gate, immersed in reminiscence of long ago and far away, enjoying wickedness and power, an old plaything of God like Sarah or Job. On yet another morning I awaken in fullness of my character and all the days of my life, tearful, grateful, and satisfied. My complexity cannot be reduced to any one of these strands. To be only a mean old man, or always a list of complaints, or a record-breaking centenarian of 105, or a head flowing with long white hair and issuing long tales of cautionary experiences is to reduce the uniqueness of character to the unity of a caricature. The Bible does not allow that monistic mistake.

II

LEAVING

The afternoon knows
what the morning never suspected.

Swedish proverb

CHAPTER 4

From "Lasting" to "Leaving"

All aboard!

T
he move from lasting to leaving changes our basic attitude from holding on to letting go. It is a major paradigm shift, a movement of archetypes. Lasting has sustained us because it expresses the instinct of self-preservation said to be the "first law of nature." It feels as if life itself wants to last and wants us to go on and on. Under the dominance of lasting, we feel leaving to be a defeat. The inevitable has arrived; leaving can mean one thing only: dying.

But what dies? You are still here, still feeling and thinking, having your breakfast in the midst of your days, not at all dying and certainly not dead.

What is dying, however, is the commitment to holding on to those attitudes that belong to lasting and that have preserved us so far. As the archetypal base of these attitudes departs, we feel ourselves unsupported, susceptible to all sorts of unfamiliar incursions, and in decline. Anything strange in our minds or habits we at once attribute to aging and dying. Our former sustaining idea of "holding on" had aimed to keep death on the other side of the wall. So if lasting is no longer the archetypal paradigm, then we have opened the door to death. That is why it is so hard to set aside the advice given us daily by those internalized coaches, the aerobic exercise director and the octogenarian Bulgarian goatherd: Keep active, walk uphill, eat yogurt, do your chores, practice your motor skills, work out, develop new interests and friends, don't worry, laugh, think positive. Try harder, do more. Last!

I think this is a gross and widespread misunderstanding of what is going on. The transition from lasting to leaving is first of all psychological, and to me it means this: It is not we who are leaving, but a set of attitudes and interpretations regarding the body and the mind that have outlasted their usefulness—and their youthfulness. We are being forced to leave them behind. They can no longer sustain us, not because we are old, but because *they* are old. The need to hold on becomes a regressive resistance, spawned by fear of dying more than by zest for living. Because our bodies and our minds are functioning in ways that our previous attitudes cannot comprehend, we see only dysfunction, decay, and death. Therefore the fear; therefore the hatred of what is happening in us, to us, and the hatred of ourselves, our hearts, our sex, our skin, our bones, and our changing souls. Therefore we wish to set back the clock and keep lasting as our ruling principle.

The more we try to last, the more afraid we become, for we are going against the innate intelligence of human nature. To go against the rules of our own intelligence dumbs us down and fulfills the physiological expectations that we will have slower faculties in later years. Yes, faculties are changing, but it is the attitude toward these changes that convinces us of dumbing and slowing. Trying to last produces the very conditions we are trying to hold off by lasting—a self-defeating strategy that leads to a self-fulfilling prophecy: older age as slow decay.

When I think of my physiology as my inmost "nature," I will be on the watch for decline from day to day. What keeps me lasting will be those baneful familiars: Hypochondria, Obsession, Anxiety, and Depression. The scale, the diet, the mirror, and the toilet bowl become my fetish companions. If I can instead think of my inmost "nature" as my character, I may turn to the changes in my nature with a curious mind, digging for discoveries. I can study these changes for insights into character, rather than measuring them against models from the past.

Physiological models for understanding changes perhaps best suit the earlier years, when growth is paramount. Then, we were more driven by the selfish gene—the current phrase for the old instinct of self-preservation—which pushes us to last and come out on top. Over time, however, the importance of physiological models diminishes. Physiology—the brain, the circulation, the joints—remains undeniably important, but as an explanatory model for understanding later life it declines in power. Its explanations limp; its insights dim. It can't tell us enough. "The enigma of aging is that it is expressed in each one of us but its underlying nature remains a mystery," concludes the eminent physiologist and professor of reproductive biology Roger Gosden.[1] To account for this mystery, more than three hundred theories of aging have been listed and categorized.[2]

When the paradigm shifts, the question "What is healthy for my nature?" is transformed into "What is important for my character?" As character comes increasingly to the fore, the "selfish gene" theory seems less adequate, because it proposes only one purpose for all life: perpetuation of genes. In later years feelings of altruism and kindness to strangers play a larger role, as if psychological and cultural factors redirect, even override, genetic inheritance and its aim of propagation. Character begins to govern life's decisions ever more pertinently, and permanently. Values come under more scrutiny, and qualities such as decency and gratitude become more precious than accuracy and efficiency.

The transition in meaning of "inmost nature" from structures of physiology to structures of character makes more livable sense of later years. Yet gerontology continues to focus on the biology of aging, and so does not come to honest terms with the character of the elderly. A science of aging that starts in the physiology of change rather than in its significance for the individual is not speaking to the aging person.

Suppose we agree that the various kinds of scientific reduction (molecular biology, information theory, evolutionary psychology) account for human aging, and that therefore questions about its meaning and purpose are mere smoke and mirrors, attempts to escape the scientific facts. But speculative and philosophical questions arise in the human mind, especially the aging mind, and deserve respect on the level at which they are posed. They need answers in kind, even if their legitimacy cannot be admitted by the models of thought that rule the scientific reductions.

When Avram Goldstein, a pioneer among brain researchers, says "it is not a question of psychology *versus* biology; on the contrary, in the final analysis (but our present knowledge falls far short) psychology *is* biology," he is reducing what matters most in later years to a way of thinking that belongs more to earlier years.[3] Earlier years must focus on getting things done, while later years consider what was done and how.

It is said that the science of aging is a young science; "gerontology" is a twentieth-century word. Gerontology is new in its methods and youthful in its progressivist hopes; its researchers tend to be young. If the field that studies old age is influenced by the archetype of youth, will it not aim to retard or reverse aging rather than discover more of its significance? Will its research not be tilted against what it is looking at?

The progress individuals go through in older age, from physiology to character, requires a similar shift, a revolution even, in old-age studies. Just as the elderly leave the concrete programs of youthful aspiration for deliberative reflections, often metaphorical and meditative, so, in order to do justice to its subject, the study of later years must explore beyond the models and attitudes of science. This kind of study has been performed by recent humanist writers on aging, such as Robert Butler, Simone de Beauvoir, Anne Wyatt-Brown, and Kathleen Woodward. They are continuing the thoughtful tradition, stretching back to antiquity, of insight into the profound importance of old age, insight presented in the works of novelists, essayists, philosophers, artists—and physicians, too.

This shift toward a humanist study of aging implies an abandonment of the worldview that commands the resources for aging research. Instead, we should fund what more likely nourishes older years: companionship, freedom, all the arts, nature, silence, service, simplicity, and safety.

In trying to last, we seek to extend life. It is equally important to extend our understanding of life: life as it is, not as it was; life structured with intelligence; life as instruction.

In old age, interest shifts from information to intelligence. By this I mean that information brings news, while intelligence searches it for insight. The data say your hearing, your eyesight, your joints are not what they were. They are not lasting. What intelligence can be garnered from this information? What insights can make later years more intelligent? "I am dying" could be said at any age, and though oppressively ponderous and certainly true, it is a truism and not particularly intelligent. Besides, if lasting continues to be paramount, information merely accumulates; it must be filed, sorted, indexed, revised. Insights last.

The practical mind usually lacks this insight. It pours the streams of consciousness directly into concrete forms. It makes an idea quickly literal, so that it can be put straight to use. This practical approach, also called instrumentalism, prevails in the young and among those still climbing; it seems also to dominate physiological gerontology. The bodily fact that I cannot pick up, as I once could, the fifty-pound feed bag, heave the suitcase onto the overhead rack, or lift the planter onto the porch railing signifies a concrete, measurable decline in my capacity, perhaps reversible with corrective exercises and anti-arthritic treatment. It is a literal problem to be resolved by concrete methods.

Suppose that, rather than seeking bodily explanation, I read these changes in my lifting capacity more reflectively, as bodily expression. "Am I picking up more than I should be? What am I carrying around—big responsibilities, leaden feelings, over-stuffed baggage? Perhaps I've piled up so much that only by becoming unable on one level to take on more will I be forced to examine what's already on my back, or discover another kind of capacity to carry. Do I have to put my hands on everything? Or can I now have a different firmness of grip, coming from the authority of a firmer character? If there are still concrete tasks to be done, are there other ways of doing them? Admitting the need for help, for instance, or collaborating, pacing, timing, lightening up, cutting myself some slack, or closing down on new efforts so as to relish earlier accomplishments?"

In later years the body works its wisdom in subtle ways. Its method does not seem wise at all; in fact, we feel stupid, forgetful, and impatient, afflicted with embarrassing symptoms. Our expectations of what wisdom is and how aging should progress toward this wisdom distort what we are going through. Dumbed down by our ideal of the old, wise person, we miss the forming of character that is actually taking place in these "symptoms" of aging. For that is where the wisdom lies.

Wrinkles and creases are not merely signs of aging flesh and drying skin; they display the lines of character. A stiffened neck indicates more than the erosion of cartilage and vertebrae; that neck might express a certain rigidity and headstrong stubbornness of character. The stiffness asks to be questioned: What does it have to do with unbending forwardness, with fixity of outlook; with an inability to nod assent or bow one's head; with turning away or against?

Climbing the stairs, you pause and pant. Lasting whispers: "Your lungs; the heart can't take the sudden strain; you are getting weaker every day." Leaving says: "Why are you still climbing, still pushing yourself upward, step after step? Is there no other way to reach another level?"

It would be a mistake to imagine the move from lasting to leaving as a process in time only. Of course time moves us from youth to age, even if it often does not always move our thought along as rapidly or completely. Old habits of thought hang on and are part of what makes us feel old. The voices that speak when lifting the bag or climbing the stairs occur concurrently. They represent two ways of hearing our behavior, two alternative constructions of what is happening. The one points backward, to what we were. It compares now with then—and this comparison is odious, because it levels a new event down to an old frame. The second alternative searches the symptoms for their hidden intelligence.

—

I suppose the body has something to say about leaving, and not only about its failure at lasting. This attitude saves the body's aging phenomena from being purely negative. I take myself to be a body-being whose most savvy and sustaining knowledge, often called instinct, comes from this body. Body-being, however, includes more than sheer biological being, for a body is a form, a psychic field, a house of souls who make their homes in all its rooms. As a psychic field, the physical body is a citadel of metaphors that can be read for psychological intelligence as well as for bio-information.

A psychologist looks at the messes he comes across as having some intention. What goes on in a patient may seem utterly aimless and destructive, yet we search for a hidden purpose. What do these wounds and errors signify? We assume that life is essentially intelligent, not haphazard, and therefore intelligible, not absurd. Whether our assumption is verifiable is not our concern, for we are not constrained by experimental method. However, like natural scientists, we also turn to phenomena to learn from them. Although we are aware, perhaps more than most, of the limits of consciousness and rational inquiry, we do not give up our idea of intention. We don't shirk the work of inquiry, that search for intelligence in a symptom. We refuse to finesse the obscurities in a person's character by generalizing away to some Great Bland Obscurity of the spirit—for instance, "Life is an unknowable mystery." Nor do we join the dogmatists of a single theory, such as evolutionary biology. We try to steer a course between the rock of belief and the hard-nosed place of reductive science, without being diverted by either.

So, when it comes to aging, I am led to assume that there is intelligence in life that intends aging just as it intends growth in youth. As we *un*fold into speaking, standing, walking, discriminating, and mastering, so we may *in*fold, once called the involution of aging. As we must unfold or develop to gain entry into the world, so infolding or aging is essential to our leaving. Not the leaving of life; we never leave life until life leaves us—suicide the exception. We are alive until declared dead. If dying is a possibility from the very first breath, so living endures until the very last. It is an enormous mistake to read the phenomena of later life as indications of death rather than as initiations into another way of life.

Unfolding, evolving, developing, improving. "From hour to hour, we ripe and ripe," says Shakespeare's witty aging philosopher Jaques, in *As You Like It*. "And then from hour to hour, we rot and rot." If ripening does not last into later years, then neither should its mode of thinking. Rot has its own phenomenology: decay, stagnation, desiccation, corruption, fragmentation. All are *living* processes, and we ignore their particular richness by reducing them to the one common denominator called death.

Anything we tie to death kills it. Death is a bugaboo; it conjures visions and frights so staggering that they block the work of inquiry. Some psychologists have claimed that the "denial of death" motivates much of contemporary human action, but the contrary may be more true in later years. We use the idea of death to deny further inquiry into the symptoms of old age, because we claim already to know their purpose. All the strange new phenomena supposedly point straight to death. This Great Unknown swallows up the new, the strange, the uncanny, the sudden, everything that belongs with the archetypal shift into unknown territory. "Dying" refers more to what we are leaving than to where and how we are alive now. Stranded in unknown territory, with a mainly physiological understanding of the aging process we are undergoing, our fears narrow us down and backward to the concrete practical thinking we are used to. We try to restore not only lost youth but the youthful way of explaining life. We forget that "unknown" cannot be equated with death. "Unknown" means anything and everything we simply do not know, including what is not yet known, another mode of being alive and being in life, another way to be human that has less to do with *becoming* a full man or woman than with *being* a unique character. What we call rot would be the way in which this character begins to show, and must be a very intention of character.

Shakespeare's philosopher mixes up stages and ages. When he reviews the classic stages of life from mewling infancy to toothless dotage, he seems to forget the very stage he is on, which has nothing to do with time's progress. "All the world's a stage," he says. At any age we are on this stage, entering and exiting as characters.

This transformation of thought from physiological to psychological calls for fresh language. We will need all the terms associated with character, such as "honor," "dignity," "authority," "prudence," "grace," "depth," "mercy," "courage," "constancy," "loyalty." We will think again in terms of form, style, quality, shape. ("He's in good form"; "Her style is all her own"; "She's got lots of good qualities"; "I'm in bad shape.") We will need to revive ideas like "ancestor," "matriarch," "patron," "mentor," and "crone." The words describing our approach will change: instead of "explanation," *"understanding"*; instead of "new studies," *"old texts"*; instead of "improvement," *"necessity"*; instead of "health," *"soul"*; instead of "experiment" and "statistic," *"philosophy"*; instead of "information," *"intelligence," "insight,"* and *"vision"*; and instead of "empowerment" and "entitlement," *"idiosyncrasy," "passion,"* and *"folly."*

But never would we abandon the aging body as a source of insights. The alterations of the aging body are precisely where wisdom lies. The body remains the teacher. "Behind your thoughts and feelings, my brother, there stands a mighty ruler, an unknown sage. . . . In your body he dwells; he is your body," said Nietzsche.[4]

Goldstein's arrogant declaration—"psychology *is* biology"— may now be accepted. All we need do is shift its meaning. His statement would no longer say: Your soul is reducible to and explicable by your physiology, and so all your psychological troubles can be addressed as biological problems. Now we take it to mean: Physiology is identical with soul; physiology is always psychological. Biological systems are psychological fields, asking to be read for their intelligence.

This is precisely what Part II of this book will do, in a series of short excursions. We shall read the agitations and miseries of aging for their psychological intentions, for their contributions to and insights into character. And we shall not neglect the rot, because what feels most concrete, ugly, and unacceptable offers the more surprising insights.

CHAPTER 5

Repetition

"Play it again, Sam."

R epetition is a major specialty of old age. Conventional
geriatrics links this habit to failing short-term memory:
You don't realize you're telling the same story again because you don't recall having already told it, and often. Repetition, they say, demonstrates the withering brain.

Old people repeat, almost exactly. If this is a symptom, it is
also their style. I once interrupted a garrulous uncle in his
eighties in the middle of one of his boringly familiar travel stories. "You've already told me that," I said. Quick as a wink, and
just as irritated as I, he shot back, "I like telling it." (Under his
breath he probably also said, "And what the hell is wrong with
telling it again? Don't you know anything about the pleasure of
telling the same stories?") He refused to allow the eye and ear
of youth to judge a characteristic of later years. He knew the joy
of the groove.

Repetition brings together the very old and the very young.
They share this pleasure. Why conceive of repetition as a failing rather than as a necessary component of imagination? Why
not, instead, conceive of the need for novelty as an addiction?
After all, repetition is essential to the oral tradition, to passing
on stories from generation to generation. It seems to be the

means by which the lore of the ancestors is kept alive and kept right. Why do children insist that a story be told in precisely the same way each time, and why do they want the very same story again and again? Perhaps writing had to come into the world so we could be sure that stories were repeated in a set form without oral embellishments, without novelty and variation. Repetition satisfies a longing for sameness.

When Grandmother tells yet again about the chimney fire that blazed onto the roof and almost burned the house down, and recounts how each member of the family did this and that, the story is boring only if you listen with an ear for fact. But the story is also a lesson about concealed dangers, about protecting "home," about family collaboration, and about the character of each of the "characters," whose styles emerge through the emergency.

Why must these stories be told repeatedly? What is the story trying to tell beyond Grandmother's telling, and why are grandmothers through the ages repositories of stories? These stories, repeated and repeated, over and over, show the lore-making, mythologizing function of the psyche, which turns the disasters and celebrations of the family, of the town into foundation stones that give background and underground to the patternless flow of daily events. By means of repetition the psyche forms significance from the ordinary. It is as if the soul begs for the same stories so that it knows that something will last.

Not only last, but last as a singularity, in the words of Gilles Deleuze, a French philosopher who electrifies received ideas with shocking deconstructions. Deleuze suggests that the more frequent the repetition, the more singular the phenomenon that is being repeated, for only the singular celebrates itself by repeating again and again. By "carrying the first time to the nth power," repetition artfully glorifies.[1] Repetition magnifies an event by commemorating its originality; in this repetition differs altogether from reproduction, which succeeds only in making each repetition a weaker echo, a paler print, with less and less power than the original.

According to Deleuze, repetition paradoxically establishes the unique originality of what is repeated, so that old people with their old stories celebrate the indestructible singularity of their character by their boring, repetitious expressions. Through them courses an archetypal energy—the gripping intensity of the Ancient Mariner driven, compelled to tell his story—that gives events everlasting importance. Bored as we may be with the familiar content, and annoyed by the compulsion, we are nonetheless comforted by the archetypal iteration. We do not hope for a new story, or recollect a different one, but stay captivated in an eternal sameness. Kierkegaard writes in his surprising essay "Repetition":

> Hope is a charming maiden but slips through the fingers, recollection is a beautiful old woman but of no use at the instant, repetition is a beloved wife of whom one never tires. For it is only of the new one grows tired. Of the old one never tires. When one possesses that, one is happy . . . life is a repetition and this is the beauty of life.[2]

Thus the story told yet again, and so annoyingly boring on one level, intimates the lasting stability of cosmic time. As Kierkegaard goes on to say: "The world continues, and it continues because it is a repetition." That forgetful old uncle, that tiresome grandmother offer a foretaste of the eternal. They function as ancestors, reminding us that recapitulation is the way the world really works—an idea set forth by the much neglected Italian philosopher Giambattista Vico (1668–1744), and named by him *ricorso*.

Freud tied repetition to death. He considered the desire to repeat to be an instinct, rooted in biology. This instinct's first aim is to bring back an earlier condition, so that the repeated story represents a piece of the past (though disguised), lifts repression from the past, reduces anxiety and tension. Now, asks Freud's theory, what is the very earliest condition that the instinct desires to return to by means of repetition? Answer: a prevital, inorganic condition of pure entropy, a state of nonbeing in which there is no tension whatsoever—in other words, Death. Freud called this static condition Nirvana, and the instinctual drive toward it, Thanatos. In later life, the compulsion to repeat indicates death at work in the soul, Freud would say, much as geriatric psychology asserts that repetition is one indication of the failing organism on its way to ultimate stasis.

Thus, my old uncle's irritable insistence upon repeating stories was an expression of, even evidence of, his death drive, allaying tension and anxiety, helping him to rest in peace—if we go along with a Freudian explanation. Moreover, telling those same old stories assured him he was still quite alive; for repetition, say some Freudian theorists, denies the passage of time. The tale doesn't change, so neither does the teller. Hence my uncle's compulsive need for exactitude in repetition. The joy of the groove was a way of staying alive and satisfying the death drive, both.

Suppose we remove repetition from the teller to the tale, from an instinct in the person to a power in the story, from modern psychology to archaic tradition.

Then we would have to admit that certain stories force themselves upon a teller, especially an older teller, who traditionally takes part in society on behalf of ancestors. There is a life force in the tale apart from any death drive in the teller. Once this energetic content is poeticized into a story, it tells something that must be told apart from the teller's person, something that indeed denies the passing of time and keeps the life of the soul going. That is perhaps the central message of Scheherazade. The vitality of her story kept her life going on simply by means of another never-concluding chapter.

Barry Lopez puts it like this:

> The stories people tell have a way of taking care of them. If stories come to you, care for them. And learn to give them away where they are needed. Sometimes a person needs a story more than food to stay alive. That is why we put these stories in each other's memory. This is how people care for themselves.[3]

Because repetition is so tedious, we have gone far out for inspiration from philosophers so that we can lift it from banality.

Nothing more tedious than practicing your scales or mumbling your beads. Yet the accomplishments of art, the efficacy of prayer, the beauty of ritual, and the force of character depend on petty repetitions any instant of which, taken for itself alone, seems utterly useless.

Gravity's Sag

London Bridge is falling down,
falling down, falling down.
London Bridge is falling down,
my fair lady.

The contrast between youth and age shows clearly in the shift from ascending to declining. The biology of younger times is a biology of literal "growing up." The spine extends with resilient cartilage packed between the vertebrae; bones elongate. In later years, the pull of gravity takes over. Ambitious, upwardly mobile social climbing, career and class, no longer offer glamour. You no longer need to be among the beautiful people or stand on the top deck shouting orders. Instead, the Great Sag: eye pouches, double chins, jowls, pendent breasts, hanging skin on upper arms, droopy belly, butt, scrotum, labia; even the earlobes grow long toward the floor. The gaze is downward; we lower our head to watch our step. "I grow old, I grow old / I shall wear the bottom of my trousers rolled," says the inward-turning, life-refusing J. Alfred Prufrock in T. S. Eliot's famous poem.[1]

In Japan, bowing the upper body is not simply a mannered postural greeting, a show of deference. It is also a practice that builds the ancestor into one's framework. Old people are supposed to be bent over like stalks of ripe rice. Our culture sees only osteoporosis. We see the body, but not its instruction. Or we get one bare message only: We're heading for the grave.

Buried within "grave" are four distinct meanings: gravity, the mysterious physical force that draws all things down to the core of the earth; gravitas, the Roman word for weighty seriousness; the grave of the cemetery, where the body is laid to final rest; and gravid, pregnant (as we once said, "heavy with child").

Since words have their way with us, these meanings tend to fuse in our minds, violating the mental Puritanism that strives to keep terms separated by clean definitions, uncontaminated with suggestive implications. Since these four meanings can fuse, worries in older age may also be about the grave of death, about the weighty seriousness and implacable downward demand of the core. The downward pull makes us anxious. Focusing on the cemetery, waiting for it, more likely displaces more serious matters: the depths of *gravitas* and the invisible pregnancy that the aged are meant to bear. We old ones are the weight bearers, and nature grows us downward.

In later years, our reach into the world has a short horizon. Think globally, yes—but only *think* globally. Despite the cruises and campers, the action is local. We are back in the neighborhood, as custodian. In our later years, we pull in the outposts. At ten, fantasy drives an exploring module around the moon; at twenty, the Trans-Siberian Railway or hunkering down to help natives in Mindanao; at thirty, a year off in Tuscany or Tahiti. We station a couple of scouts at the perimeter of the empire—geographical, and also intellectual. We shall take music lessons, learn Spanish dance, paint on a houseboat, read Proust, Gibbon, and Cervantes, open a restaurant, write a movie script or a detective novel, study Chinese, play the commodities markets. We begin to send a few more troops to these outposts, visit them, dwell there. We gather clippings, keep notes and addresses, mark possible future dates in the calendar. Then, as years pass, we begin to call the troops home, one by one. With lingering nostalgia we abandon them to the sands and the wind, traceless fantasies. Some vanish without yearnings, more likely with amazement that they once seemed viable parts of the empire. Pulling in the outposts is simply calling home the possibilities and dropping into where you are, your place.

I tie the sag, the dropping and drooping of body parts to a

homing instinct. The home aimed for is not only here where you are, but farther down than the grave itself: the underworld beneath the grave, which can be entered long before the actual grave in the actual cemetery. So many of the great mythical figures—Ulysses, Aeneas, Inanna, Hercules, Psyche, Orpheus, Persephone, Dionysos—descended and gained a knowledge that deepened their characters. Psyche in the underworld grasped a kind of beauty that is invisible; Hercules' character had to enlarge to take in realities that are not physical. Inanna "gave ear" to things unknown in the upper world. Aeneas, like Dante, met bodiless forms with no substance yet with terrifying power and bearing the names of the soul's pains and evils. Unlike Jesus' descent, intended to eliminate the deeps and undertaken by one who had no late years, no old age, the downward move of these figures is essential to the long-lasting power of their stories and their characters. Dionysos has a somber side pictured by his black beard and recognized in his mysteries; Ulysses goes home to wife and son a war-wearied man; Psyche's pregnancy comes to term; Persephone passes a good part of the year below, married to the invisible. The ability of these mythologized persons to get down added to their lasting gravitas, enabling them as ancestors of our culture to carry weight through the ages.

Growing down into the world by becoming useful to it and helping shape it requires getting down below the world. To be an elder, benefactor, conservator, and mentor calls for a learning about shadows, an instruction from the "dead" (that is, from what has gone before, become invisible, yet continues to vivify our lives with its influences). The "dead" come back as ancestors, especially in times of crisis, when we are at a loss. Then the dead "awaken," offering a deeper knowledge and support. They have already fallen; they know the pits, hence their enormous resources. They do not have to return as literal voices and visions, for they are already palpable in whatever is pulling us down, wherever we can't keep up. They are the force in the psyche's gravity.

As Heraclitus said: "Underworld souls perceive by smelling." Twenty-five hundred years later, we say that the person who can get down has a quick apprehension—"street smarts"—and senses reality behind the front. Ancient descriptions of the underworld maintain that in this realm nothing solid exists, only images, phantoms, ghosts, smoke, mist, shades, dreams. We cannot see it; we can only see into it, with suspicions, hunches, intuitions, feelings. It is a two-dimensional realm with no more—and no less—substance than words, feelings, thoughts, reflections.

The old have gravitas when their insight reaches into the invisible core of things, into what is hidden and buried. These graver, pregnant meanings are not advertised in the daily round. The old hear into the gaps, smell what's not kosher, watch for small smiles that disguise the truth—all the necessary suppressions that make every day possible, and nice. When the body begins to sag, it is abandoning sham and hypocrisy. The body leads the way down, deepening your character. It doesn't know how to lie.

This may account for some of the nastiness of old people, their thriving on wicked stories and twisted gossip, on surgical mistakes and bad doctors, crooked relatives, scandals, accidents, and ruined finances. They are tuned in to the underworld, so they go to sleep reading crime novels and watching cop flicks. They enjoy the vicious psychopathy of the heroes and heroines of afternoon soaps and the bizarre pathologies exhibited on talk shows. They are more at home in the underworld of peculiarities than in the conventions of conformity.

We like to idealize elders. We expect gravitas from them, benign wisdom. But these expectations are illusions unless we realize that this wisdom is on display in their bodies' deformations, when these deformations are read less through geriatric physiology than through imaginative psychology. Aging makes metaphor of biology. The organic changes are a form of poetic speech, rewriting personality into character.

CHAPTER 7

Waking at Night

. . . hate to see the evenin' sun go down,
Makes me think I'm on my last go-round.

W. C. Handy,
"St. Louis Blues"

W hy do old people sleep less at night and slip into little naps in broad daylight, dozing off in the midst of company? Why this reversal of conventional sleeping habits? Unlike the young, who can zone out and lie comatose right up until lunch, we lie awake in the dark and doze off in daylight. With the years, normal sleep gradually dwindles from the prescribed eight hours to six, even five. Night more and more becomes our time. Against our will, the ancient goddess Nyx (Night) is forcing us to become her devotees.

So much goes on at night; not only dreams and reminiscences and prayers; not only fears, those visiting demons who sit at the edge of your bed and recount your blunders and worries, and then fly off (as vampires do) once morning finally comes. Even more insistent are pressing toilet calls.

In early years the involuntary urge to urinate does not disturb sleep. Small children can wet their beds without waking, so strong is the child's need to stay asleep and to protect this sleep from waking in the night, with its often fearful intruders. In late years, however, the urge to urinate interferes with sleep, as if the wisdom of the older body calls you to wake up.

Bladder calls at night affect daytime living, too. You must

watch your evening fluid intake, avoid diuretics, plan ahead for stops when traveling. More and more nighttime creeps into the day. In stark physical terms, we feel trapped in a body over which we are losing control and whose nightly message is decay.

Suppose, however, that getting up from sleep awakens you not only *in* the night, but *to* the night. Once, in monasteries and nunneries, night watch was called vigil, and sleep was shortened on purpose so that when the Lord of Temptations came calling and his minions tried to enter your thoughts at night you could ward them off. The early Christian monks who lived in desert caves tried to banish sleep altogether, since pagan powers were thought to approach pious souls through dreams. Moreover, since the visionary book of Revelation says "there shall be no night there" in the kingdom to come, some religious orders have sought to approach that eternal day by literally banning sleep. So the devout person intent upon building a strong character was less eager to sleep than to keep watch at night. Character depended on fending off the fantasies and voices that threatened to lead one away from the Christian path. To fend them off, the devout had to open their eyes to the night so as to discriminate among the spirits.

Awakening to the night opens a dark eye into the invisible world. It opens an acute ear to cautions, insights, and promptings that seem to visit only at night, disturbing sleep in order to be heard. We hardly suffer from the same crowd of anxieties and reconstructed nostalgic longings in daylight.

This crowd of spirits that we call worry, self-castigation, anxiety, remorse, death terror, and erotic longing had similar names in the old world of the Mediterranean. For us they are psychological abstractions; for the ancients they were personified figures, children of Nyx. We can see these "invisible" persons, Night's offspring, painted on vases and carved in relief: fatalistic foreboding (*moros*), fault-finding (*momos*), punishers (*keres*) and avengers (*nemesis*), angry persecutors (*erinyes*), miserable distress (*oizys*) and lustful longings (*kupris*). The Bible calls Nyx by another name, Lilith, the night-monster "roaming with her retinue in the darkest hours of the night."

Of course, Nyx had another side, a happier function. She brought ease to the weary, and her wide dark wings spread protectively over the sleeping world. In later years however, the shelter she affords interests us less than that crowding in of her plaguing offspring who demand we wake up in the dead of night.

Waking up to these figures of the night world deepens and broadens character. You come to know what cannot enter during the day, what Freud called the repressed. Dreams (also children of Nyx, according to the old myths) are not enough to return the repressed to awareness, for, as Freud said, their function is to protect sleep. And dreams do mostly let us sleep peacefully, by masking our worries and terrors and presenting them in the guise of images we do not understand, letting us dream on without waking.

But to dream on without waking seems not to be what aging physiology wants. Not only do the bladder, the sphincter, and the enlarged prostate play their roles in getting men out of bed at night, but so does a strange, newly studied change in circadian rhythm. Research on men in Denmark and Japan shows that something happens to the younger, habitual patterns of urine production. "Healthy young adults produce urine three times faster during the day than at night." Although the older men in these studies produced the same total amounts of urine as younger men in any twenty-four-hour period, older men were no longer retaining salt and water during the night; they were instead excreting more sodium at night, and thus voiding more frequently. The report concludes by saying that "some people with nocturia have disordered circadian rhythms," and "there's not much you can do to regulate your body's clock."[1]

There is, however, something you can do about *understanding* your body's clock. Men are being forced to learn another rhythm. (Women were not included in these studies, initiated as inquiries into prostate disorders and repairs.) The biological clock "intends" to rouse us elders from sleep and awaken us to the darkness around us. Plato called for this awakening from darkness, in his famous allegory of the cave. The concluding two stanzas of one of William Stafford's finest poems about the erosion of character due to careless inattention puts it like this:

And so I appeal to a voice, to something shadowy,
a remote important region in all who talk:
though we could fool each other, we should consider—
lest the parade of our mutual life get lost in the dark.

For it is important that awake people be awake,
or a breaking line may discourage them back to sleep;
the signals we give—yes or no, or maybe—
should be clear: the darkness around us is deep.[2]

Evidently we sleep less in later years because our tasks change. If once we were to be sheltered by Night herself, now we must learn from her offspring. Phantoms of Fate, Death, Despair, Blame, Revenge, and Desire won't let you rest. You have to discriminate among the invisible figures who share your home, even your bed. Letting them awaken you, receiving their biting attacks, and studying the legitimacy of their claims—this is hard work. An hour or two with the children of Nyx, wide-eyed in a dark room, can be exhausting. Little wonder that some eighty different sleep disorders have been catalogued and that there are 337 sleep disorder clinics in the United States. Ten percent of the population report a nightmare at least once a month. Little wonder, then, that so many of us take sleeping pills and wear incontinence pads so that we can rise in the morning without having had to tangle with (and learn from) the persecutory brood of Nyx.

I do believe she wants us to know her better. Perhaps she takes offense at our methods of avoiding knowledge of the night. Our culture's light pollution and its after-dark noise levels may be offensive to her; who knows? What place outdoors and nearby is free of artificial light and the sounds of civilization? How far do we have to travel to look up to a full sky of stars? What do you or I know about differentiating Night, beyond divisions into prime time, late night, and bedtime. Do we know Night's sounds and smells, where the constellations are, the moon's condition, the soughing of the wind at dawn, how the house rattles and settles?

Besides the animal creatures that thrive on the night's black air; besides thieves, third-shift workers, jazz players, street-walkers, and other nightcrawlers, all invisible in the daytime—besides these, inanimate things come alive in the dark, as so many fairy tales and ghost stories tell children. The restless mind is besieged by insights; lying sleepless, we develop a strange intelligence. Is this how the images of the dead communicate, how the ancestors instruct us? Many indigenous peoples wait until nightfall to sacrifice to ancestor spirits and to feast and dance to propitiate their fearful powers. Keeping vigil to know the night was one way of gaining strength from the invisible world. Specific rituals belong to different phases of the night, as if the night had a variety of faces. In medieval Japan there were clocks that told time by releasing smells: every two hours a different odor wafted through the air, so that on waking in the dark you could literally sense what time it was. For us, Night is mostly all the same: In our blinds-drawn room, we little know or care whether what we awaken to is the darkness of midnight, three A.M., or just before daybreak. No patrolling watchman calls the hours, no bells peal from the towers and steeples. Yet the body has its timekeeper, and nurses on night-duty know to expect certain crises in different patients at particular hours.

We do not distinguish the parts of the night because we have yoked Nyx to day-world duties. We go to bed for oblivion, not for worry. Nighttime is for catching up on sleep, for being recharged for tomorrow, which will take off, manic: we'll needle our scalps with a quick hot shower, followed by a jolt of juice, some cheery pops and snaps, a mug of sugared caffeine—rituals to ban the last traces of Nyx and her brood and the sleeping drugs we have taken to keep her at bay.

If character is fate, and if the Fates as avengers and pursuers are daughters of Night, then character building may need the physiological changes that awaken the old into night. What else could so urgently get us up? It seems character has underpinnings that sink into a dark intelligence, an intelligence that settles into us in darkness and deepens our imagination of human life, its obscure obsessions, its irrational panics. Late in the night, we realize that the acts of our lives have not been shadow-free, that we are shadowed by curses and sins—not because we are cursed and sinful by nature, but because with the very origin of the world, one half of which belongs to Night, come fearful figures who demand we know them. All you know of the day world is only half-knowledge. Character asks for a larger truth, a richer understanding, and the beginning of this wisdom is imparted by these dreadful visitations.

How does this wisdom bear on character? First, you learn that your emotions are not quite yours; they are not so much to be controlled as to be reckoned with. Fatalistic anxieties, recriminations, and vengeful afterthoughts that come *in* the night come *from* the night. They derive neither from your brain and its processes nor from your personality and its behaviors. They belong instead to the dark, impersonal underside of the world, which becomes personally available to you through the ordeal of nighttime awakenings.

Second, because your heart turns so cold and beats so wildly, you have to take to heart old lessons that once seemed only Sunday sermons and philosophical theories, such as Kierkegaard's and Heidegger's primacy of dread, such as the biblical God's insistence that fear is the beginning of wisdom, such as that God's terrifying wrath against peoples, cities, and nations and his persecutory manipulation of even his good servant Job.

Third, you grasp something of the hellish reality of the realm of shades, an underworld essential to so many mythologies, religions, and rituals of initiation, and to the making of art. The dreadful masks of ancestors and tribal spirits exhibited in exotic anthropological collections become actual dark angels inhabiting your own room. Enduring their attacks takes character.

CHAPTER 8

Muddled Agitation

All human evil comes from this,
man's inability to sit still in a room.
Pascal

Two days ago becomes two months ago. The day nurse is the night nurse. Where you have been and where you want to be or have never been can equally complete your sentence because tenses no longer follow the laws of grammar. You are in a suppositional present where what might and what did and what should lose their distinctions. You have entered a time-free zone, a state of being that the French anthropologist Lucien Lévy-Bruhl called a "primitive mentality" and "prelogical" consciousness. Your book of life has lost its page numbers, even its punctuation. Life as a run-on sentence, with ellipses, lacunae, iterations that can be read any which way, backward as good as forward. Phrases break off. You stamp your foot to bring back the thought. What was I telling you? The thread, the thread . . .

To pick it up, you pick yourself up. You go get something. What you are going to get and where you are going are indefinite, but the wandering body is following the agitations of the wandering mind, and getting into trouble. Here's where the falls begin, the accidents. They say, "Why can't he just stay put!" They don't understand that staying put spins you yet further into the agitation of the muddle.

The names of family members muddle and merge. These familiar people come visiting and "not for the life of you" can you keep them straight. Everyone looks so different from your image of them—and these images must be the true record, since they have stood the test of time. They have stayed the same in your mind's eye all these years. So you call your daughter by your sister's name, and run through four other names before hitting upon your sister. "It doesn't matter," they say. "Don't get worked up."

In a sense it really *doesn't* matter, because the muddle reflects the merging of generations into a composite image. The confusion is the result of a fusion. You have somehow merged with the family tree, seeing its various twigs and branches from the perspective of the central trunk. A similar force runs through all; all members share a generic denominator. Differences have faded. The all-at-once prevails over separation into generations. You have drifted outside the time-bound "who begat whom," older and younger, then and now.

This, too, is a wisdom. Sir Francis Galton, a cousin of Darwin and a pioneer of experimental psychology and the study of heredity, assembled hundreds and hundreds of carefully taken photographs of faces from the same families. In an early attempt at composite portraiture, he superimposed the images. The process reinforced basic features, while individual differences receded. Common characteristics superseded individual variety. By muddling differences among the individuals of the family we may be getting closer to what we essentially share with them. The apple does not fall far from the tree, but first you have to see the tree.

Much of our adult life is busy with differentiation. St. Paul considered discrimination a valuable virtue. Jung defined individuation as a process of differentiation: differentiation of consciousness, differentiation of self from collective. As mother's helpers in the supermarket, we are trained early to tell one brand from another. Not to spot the difference between one car and another, one rock band and another is a sign of slow development. From the beginning we have to tell a 3 from an 8, a 6 from a 9, pink from orange, and oranges from apples.

The release from this effort may be one of the major bless-
ings of aging, affording it an entirely outsider's kind of wisdom.
But we don't ease into this blessing, this wisdom, without some
agitation. You try vainly to regain the facility that puts a name to
a face, to walk to the right door, to match a pair among the
socks. When muddling begins, agitation follows. You feel like a
child who can't do it right, like an adult who is slipping. But
you are not a clumsy child or an impaired adult. Like an ancestor you are beginning to grasp the world less personally, re-
sponding to impersonal and lasting essentials. When I was an
adult, I spoke as an adult, I felt as an adult, I thought as an adult;
now that I am become an ancestor I have put away all adult
bothers. I will be agitated because the newspaper was brought
in late, but I don't care or even notice that it is yesterday's edition.

CHAPTER 9

Drying Up

Dry souls are wisest and best.

Heraclitus

With advancing age your nose may drip and your eyes tear in the cold, yet the membranes are actually drying. So are your scalp and skin. Body hair and cuticles grow crisper, and it's rare to work up a sweat. While youth battles oily acne and clammy palms, the old lady creams her face at night and extends a dry hand.

Early Greek medicine declared that youth was moist, while aging moved us toward the opposite pole of the fundamentals of temperament: from the hot to the cold, from the moist to the dry. We become stiff, brittle, and rigid instead of drippy, sappy, and green. The language of folk medicine continued these ancient medical ideas for many centuries. It was said that old people especially need steam baths, and tender meats from moist animals like hare and calf, as well as stews, custards, and soups. These would counter the desiccation of old age. Drying so belongs to the idea of aging that in some languages the word for old is "dry," "dry" and "old" having an identical meaning.

How little they are in their beds! The old seem to shrivel away. The littleness of the body in very old age, together with its large burden of bodily aches and dysfunctions, is less a paradox than a paradigm. It attests to the shrinking role of the body.

Its value declines in the consideration of lasting things. Conditions you imagine to be unbearable, the very old often dismiss as a bother and a bore.

Why should the body dry, and why is the dry soul "wisest and best"? Are we merely turning into juiceless mummies with parchment skin? Can we bring to this natural process a more metaphorical understanding so that desiccation means something more than old-age crustiness, another impairment on the path to death? Suppose drying is imposed on us not only by the nature of nature but by the nature of character as well. Could the wisdom of the body require desiccation?

For Heraclitus the soul was not a misty, cloudy notion or a flow of feeling. For him it was fiery, and like fire it wanted to ascend. What was best for the soul—his word for "best" was *aristos,* the root of our "aristocrat"—was more refined, more subtle, lighter and drier. Originally, the contrast between *aristos* and *hoi polloi* was cosmological. The word *polloi,* which came to be associated with the masses, is cognate with words for "flow," "moist," "pollution," "swamp," that is, the damp end of the spectrum. It is wisest and best to hold to the dry end, and therefore Heraclitus could also say, "It is death for souls to become moist."

Of course, today we cannot read this archetypal scale without reacting in terms of caste and class. We no longer have an archetypal sense of the soul and of the world to give a cosmological meaning to conditions that seem to us only symptoms, prejudices, and problems.

Anyway, a damp soul with its sloppy thinking and gushy feeling bogs us down, occludes the brightness of vision and softens the edge of decision. The dry soul reaches up, seeks illumination. It sparks with flashes of insight and quickly catches fire. And it brings light, as elder, as mentor. But wisdom seems to require some wizening.

If the old ones in a civilization are meant to act as its teachers, then they are the light keepers, the enlighteners whose wisdom can see into the dark. Their characters must carry a fire. Therefore they must be dry.

Alchemical psychology, based in the same tradition of metaphorical understanding, followed this way of thinking. Chemical stuffs were also the stuff of the psyche and had psychological meanings. Alchemists were workers in metaphor, like good psychoanalysts, and also like poets and painters.

One of the main alchemical operations employed a flat evaporating pan to steam off excess wetness so that a dry remainder could be used for further concoctions. Too much liquid and the soul substance tends to putrefy. You feel yourself swamped, flooded; can't get out of this mood; stagnating. Dissolved in grief, in yearning, in messy, sticky situations. Evaporation lets off the steam, boils away the moisture that has kept you stuck. Old glue dries to dust; you no longer adhere to former allegiances. Once the emotion is extracted from a memory, it can pass in review as an interesting curiosity. All the turbulence has evaporated, leaving bare bones, a dried essence, much like a chemical residue cleansed of extraneous matter. The reduction of the past to dry facts yields the salt of wisdom that the old are supposedly able to dispense. They only achieve these salty and bitterly true insights after their own emotional involvement has dried up.

Things drift by without comment, even without notice; it is as if the pressure to engage evaporates. The old have a more distant gaze; and though the retina may not be detached, the vision is. We have to hold things farther and farther from us in order to see them clearly. The dryness of long-distance vision. The body's own mode of Buddhist detachment.

Those strange old alchemists with their funny hats and beards and secretly coded writings seem to me to be teaching a necessary discipline of the soul: It must dry out the freshets of naive enthusiasms and overflows of sentimentality. The dried soul has a dry humor and a dry wit, a dry eye that sees the world with less subjective affections. We become astringent—sec, like a good wine.

CHAPTER 10

Memory: Short-Term Loss, Long-Term Gain

I don't know that I said that or not, ah, I really don't.

Ronald Reagan

Foolish not to know whether you already took your pills or not. As to remembering names, dates, words . . . going once, going twice, gone forever. On the one hand, brain cells may be flaking off like autumn leaves in a deciduous forest; on the other hand, a clearing is being made, leaving more space for occasional birds to alight.

The brain is conventionally and conveniently held responsible for memory loss:

> For every decade after age fifty, the brain loses 2 percent of its weight. . . . The motor area of the frontal cortex loses between 20 and 50 percent of its neurons; the visual area in the back loses about 50 percent; the physical sensory part on the sides also loses about 50 percent.

Yet parallel with this rapid deterioration of substructures, something else is going on:

> The higher intellectual areas of the cerebral cortex have a significantly lower degree of cell disappearance. . . . It may even be that the fewer neurons increase their activity. . . . Recent re-

search suggests that certain cortical neurons seem actually to become *more abundant* [my italics] after maturity. . . . the filamentous branchings (dendrites) of many neurons continue to grow in healthy old people. . . . Neuroscientists may actually have discovered the source of the wisdom which we like to think we can accumulate with advancing age.[1]

Surely one of the remarkable feats of the older mind is its ability to divide memory into two sorts: long-term and short-term. As the first improves, the latter dwindles. While you can bring back the dresses of your girlhood friends of seventy years ago, you can't find the glasses that you set down "somewhere, this very minute."

Could this division have some wisdom in it? Could the mind be refusing to take in new stuff so that images of long ago and far away can rise up in strength and freshness? It may be annoying to you and infuriating to others that you let the kettle boil away, mislay your keys, forget your great-nephew's name, but is character built of kettles and keys and the names of little boys?

Rather, character consists in deposits, especially the deposits that error and misfortune have left behind in memory and that we work over in later years. A life has a huge inventory, and whoever is the warehouse keeper runs a LIFO system—last in, first out—swiftly ridding the premises of new input in order to preserve enough emotional space for evaluating what has been there for a long time. The inability to recall this morning's conversation, let alone last week's visitors, keeps the shelves open for assembling the records so long stored.

Geriatric psychology finds that older people spend more and more time taking stock, doing their "life review." This is a work of recovery not *from* the past but *of* the past, a work of research—a *"recherche du temps perdu,"* as Proust called his massive, exquisite treatise on remembering. If past time is not to be lost time, one must give it presence. Therefore, new events come in only when they tie in with old ones. You travel to a foreign city and find yourself talking about another place it reminds you of; you meet a younger relative, and notice only the traits of her mother and aunts, who attended your wedding; you are served a special dish, only to tell how you used to make it. It is not the taste of the new dish or the face of the new relative that matters; only that they prompt old memories.

Does this imply that old people are self-centered? I think not, certainly not more so than young people, or than they themselves were in their youth. The ingathering of old images to the exclusion of recent events seems imposed on the aged, as if the soul insists on this review. As we age, something in us wants to return to distant halls and dusty mirrors. I think character wants to understand itself, increase its insight and intelligence.

We return also to commemorate. We lay wreaths and place flowers on events that left a mark. The past lies under graves, buried, but the memory of these moments in our soul history keeps their values alive. Character consolidates by commemorating moments of value in oneself. If we do not remember beautiful, courageous, honorable events, if we never recall the clarity of a decision or the cost of a sacrifice, may we assume they are still active in us unconsciously? Old age gives time to commemorate our achievements, and also our inheritance from those who taught us or were simply glad to see us. These commemorative visits to incidents of value mean we need less present praise and depend less on others for recognition. You can hold your own victory parades, award your own medals of honor.

Needing less, depending less also means being less lonely and more dignified. To have dignity in old age, to leave with dignity, belongs to a character that asks for a nobler description than contemporary psychology's "empowerment." After you've left, what do you want people to say? That you coped with great courage and showed grace, goodwill, and humor, or that you had high "self-esteem" and complete "self-realization"?

In later years, recent events, precisely because they are new, are not enough to satisfy the demands of character. Novelty attracts less and less. Life review attempts to turn events into experiences, to draw out their emotion and gather them into patterns of meaning. "It seems, as one becomes older, / That the past has another pattern, and ceases to be a mere sequence," wrote T. S. Eliot. *Four Quartets,* which meditates on time, age, and memory, goes on to say, "We had the experience but missed the meaning, / And approach to the meaning restores the experience / In a different form, beyond any meaning."[2]

I'd like to illustrate this conflict between short-term current events and long-term life review. A woman of sixty-six who was my patient supervised the care of her mother, who was in her nineties. According to my patient, the two women struggled over almost everything, sometimes bitterly, helplessly caught. Besides the conventional mother-daughter stuff and the tensions established years before, there was the actual content of their present fights. What were they about? Facts. The aged woman, though still keen, couldn't remember them, while her daughter, my patient, relentlessly corrected her on dates, appointments, names, prices, times, dosages, locations, the daily news, the whole of the short-term world par excellence. She also insisted on making it "easier" for her mother with instructions on how to use electronic devices—the answering machines, the stove timer, the VCR, the split-screen TV, the portable phone, the ice maker . . .

The old lady was half gone in reminiscence. To be brought up-to-date shut her down in an obstinate depression because her mind was in "life review," working through her storage chambers. But these phantoms, daydreams, and oft-repeated memories from the old lady's warehouse, the minor irrelevant figures long dead and insignificant to begin with, threatened my patient. Ghost stories, ancestor worship, ancient curses: every single bit of them dead. She felt her mother was lost in the past, slipping away. For my patient, to stay alive meant to stay real, that is, to keep current and concrete, and so she did her best to turn her mother's attention to the living world of fact.

I thought that my patient lacked imagination, and that I lacked the ability to awaken it in her. Then I saw psychoanalytic reasons for their fights. The daughter's lack of imagination could be understood as a fear of the unknown and uncontrollable, presented daily by the gradual disintegration of her mother. Her imagination was blocked by fear of death. And I saw other reasons, too. For instance, the mother's fixation on being "old-fashioned" and "artistic," and therefore always in need of practical direction and help, forced the daughter to be practical and helpful. Also playing its part was the daughter's sadistic use of facts to infantilize her mother by treating her as incompetent, even as losing her mind. Revenge, envy, guilt: The psychoanalyst can arrive at any scene and pull out of his bag fitting personalistic explanations. Psychoanalysis is brilliantly imaginative, despite its heavy-handed reduction of life to reasons. I want, however, to take the conflict of these women out and away from their personalities, their case histories, and away from psychoanalysis too, so we can reflect further on memory itself.

Now I can see that the conflict between my patient and her mother exemplified the difference between short-term and long-term memory. It is as if you cannot have both at once. One has to give way to the other. In young years there seems to be no place for the long term. It is hard to introduce history to school kids. Even in medical school, the history of medicine is an elective, if taught at all, whereas the latest progress and its indications for the future fill any available time for reading.

What is true of medical science may be yet more true of all the other sciences. Memory is irrelevant; worse, a burden. "History is bunk," Henry Ford is supposed to have said. The willful amnesia afflicting the sciences in general contrasts sharply with the importance given to memory by the humanities. Literature, philosophy, politics, and the visual arts, including photography and filmmaking, feed on memory. Practitioners of the humanities need memory to deepen and refine their thinking. We turn to history in this chapter for similar reasons.

For at least fifteen hundred years the term used for bringing images to mind was *memoria*. The psychology of memory, which begins with Aristotle, considered *memoria* to be absolutely fundamental to the mind. We cannot think, Aristotle said, without relying upon a collection of mental images or imagination that can be re-collected. According to this psychological tradition, what today we conventionally refer to as memory is *imagining qualified by time.* When we are recollecting, we are always imagining, even if what comes up is placed back in time. The sole difference between imagining and imagination on the one hand, and remembering and memory on the other is this added element of time.

This means that the mother in her dotage was doing more than recovering her past. She was imagining, and this world of images called her away and held her, just as her daughter said, in a realm of fantasies and phantoms. The daughter could not travel imaginatively with her mother. For her, that sort of travel was tripping out, so she felt her mother was slipping away— but, of course, the mother was only slipping away from the daughter's definition of "reality." For the very old lady, imagination in the guise of long-term remembering was real enough—and just as real as her interfering daughter.

These imaginings came to the mother with the element of time attached. They were situated in a once-upon-a-time world called the past. How much of it was accurate and how much invented we do not know, nor can we ever know this about any memory, even about short-term reporting of a recent accident, an assault or a visit by a flying saucer. Memory is always first of all imagination, secondarily qualified by time.

That the core of memory is imagination was one of Freud's most significant rediscoveries, and the one he is most pilloried for by literalists. They insist that the memory of an occurrence—for instance, a childhood sexual event—comes first even if imagination may embroider upon it. But by staying with the reality and power of the image, Freud aligned his theory with the ancient tradition of *memoria,* whose core is imagination.

Memoria helps account not only for long-term gain but also for short-term loss. We can't recall the day of the week, the nephew's name, or the corner where we must turn left. These belong to the mind's learning, and only when something learned is associated with a corresponding image does it remain available. Remembering seems to require imagination to get started. In the Renaissance, a complex systematic technique for improving memory, the *ars memoriae,* attached images to factual learning. In the absence of such images, learning fades fast. That a learned fact sticks for years and enters long-term memory indicates that it has become signified by imagination and thereby heightened in importance.

Memoria meant more than recall, more even than actively imagining and engaging with images. It was a *place,* much as we are using the term in this chapter: a storage place, a chamber, a room, a hall, a warehouse, a cavern. The older term was "thesaurus," or treasury richly packed with images. Although the entry to these rooms is through the doors of life review, collected there and available to the researching mind are "images that yet / Fresh images beget."[3] Such images aren't directly traceable to your past, your person, but are born beyond your own capacity to imagine and come on their own, like the wildest dream. St. Augustine, Keats, Coleridge, Ali Baba, Sinbad entered the cavern and were astounded.

People like to say that later years are filled with memory because the future is so short. With little to look forward to and plan for, we look back. But I am not so sure it is "we" who look back. The commemorating imagination seems to come alive on its own. We are not the sole instigators of remembering; memory seems to push itself on us, bringing for our cogitation a variety of scenes, figures, situations, images that had truly been forgotten, or that never actually happened, despite the "added element of time." Pure imaginings.

The widely reported, spontaneous appearance of images in older age, and the feeling that one has to "deal with them," make sense to me as an intention of the soul. It is as if character forces us into encounters with *memoria.* We might prefer to shop, chat on the phone, or play the slots, yet even in the mall and the motel room, the images come through, almost obsessively. We cannot escape remembering. Why? Is the brain regurgitating? Must we confess to old sins to be redeemed? Or could *memoria,* both as life review of more personal images, and as the extraordinary riches of *images themselves,* be essential to the foundation of character?

Whether the old lady was lost in the cavern and opening treasure chests of jewels that did not belong to her, or whether she was engaged in life review, something demanded her attention. Let us imagine that she was digesting. We all have to chew and swallow the errors and misfortunes, sprinkled well with the salt of remorse, of what had previously been two-dimensional memoranda, flat like pages from a calendar, simply things that happened without pattern, without meaning. Life review yields long-term gains that enrich character by bringing understanding to events. The patterns in your life become more discernible among the wreckage and the romance, more like a well-plotted novel that reveals characters through their actions and reactions. Life review is really nothing other than rewriting—or writing for the first time—the story of your life, or writing your life into stories. And without stories there is no pattern, no understanding, no art, and no character—merely habits, events passing before the eyes of an aimless observer, a life unreviewed, a life lost in the living of it.

Correctly lost, I must quickly add, for the least reflected upon, most undigested life is very much worth living—and the purpose of life in earlier years is to live it. Knowing comes later. Life review doesn't belong to earlier years. Memoirs, autobiography, and the deep investigations of long-term psychoanalysis probably shouldn't be touched before sixty. Yet kids in high school are asked to write about their memorable experiences and extract a lesson learned. Their therapies review their childhoods, which ended scarcely five years prior; their bull sessions and chat rooms focus on family difficulties and influences. Premature life review produces inflated subjectivity, not character, the empowerment of one more big fat "me" graduating from high school into a world that, already crowded with expanded egos, rather needs the modesty and reticence of the apprentice embarking on an adventure.

———

Suppose we consider life review as character making its claim. Maybe character asks not to be left unfinished, without insight into its nature, a mere jumble of unintelligible facts, a life history strung together by dates and jobs, trips and illnesses like a vast American-style biography stuffed with data and empty of conclusions. The concluding portion of life may be asking us to draw conclusions from prior actions. Could it be that the soul doesn't want to leave this world innocent of the life it has been living for ninety-odd years, and wants *memoria* to turn those years into character values?

The emergence of values from remembering repeats in our old age the ancient myth of Memory, the mother of the nine Muses. Each of the Muses—the patronesses of astronomy, comedy, dance, eloquence, epic, history, music, amatory poetry, and tragedy—artfully forms values by musing upon the goddess Memory who is her mother. We do not need to form our remembrances into art, as the painter Grandma Moses did in her old age, or into a novel, as Giuseppe di Lampedusa did in his. We need only to follow Memory's daughters, musing over our memories and noticing how they take on significant shapes.

Life review as musing doesn't have to follow a single path or come into the land of wisdom. Instead, we begin to notice each of the muses shaping our recollections. We recall epic moments, the poetic excitements of infatuation, the comedy and tragedy. We place private memories in the public history of our times, and may even imagine the role of the stars in our fate, or understand the pattern of the past as a musical composition, with themes and subthemes, or as a dance, turning and returning. Finally, we, too, may begin to tell the same detailed stories, but now with eloquence.

Freud said that stored-away mental contents do not change. They are unaffected by time. It is this pickling of the past that people find so annoying in the old. Their rooms, exterior and interior, become period museums. Preservation of the same preserves the old mind from reimagining the story and defends against musing. The divorce and its hatred, the flood and its trauma, keep imagination trapped in the literalism of "exactly as it happened." Not even moths can get at long-term memory once it is set in concrete.

Despite Freud's conviction that stored contents remain unaltered by time, I have come to believe that something does happen to them. Warmth finds its way into the cold storage vaults. In older age, the images become more pleasant. Arduous struggles, envious rivalries, even betrayals come back with a new valence. They don't hurt as much. The musing may even make them amusing. The long illness, the wrong marriage, all the slings and arrows of outrage lose their fire and forget their aim.

Why do the dark days of the past lighten up in late recollection? Is this a subtle hint that the soul is letting go of the weights it has been carrying, preparing to lift off more easily? Is this a premonition of what religious traditions call heaven, this euphoric tone now coating many of the worst experiences, so that there is little left to forgive? At the end the unforgivables will never be forgiven, because in old age they do not need to be forgiven: They have simply been forgotten. Forgetting, that marvel of the old mind, may actually be the truest form of forgiveness, and a blessing.

CHAPTER 11

Heightened Irritability

Off with their heads!
Lewis Carroll

L et's not forget that strange combination of heightened irritability and calm patience that emerges in late life. On the
one hand, older people have more passive tolerance; they will
let the day go by uselessly, put up with inconveniences, refuse
to be rushed and rattled. On the other hand, they fly off the
handle with little provocation. Nothing more than a great-
grandson's hairstyle, a late bus, a sound too loud or too low, an
inattentive waitress—and whammo, the rockets' red glare, the
bombs bursting in air.

In nursing homes, some demure elderly ladies who rarely
speak above a whisper have to be tied—not because they might
fall from their chairs and hurt themselves, but because they
pinch and punch their caretakers, so quick is their fuse, so intense their irritability.

A few centuries back, organic life at its most basic level
was thought to display its vitality through its capacity to be irritated. Albrecht von Haller, an eighteenth-century Swiss poly-
math and the "master physiologist of his time," established by
means of 567 experiments on muscle cell contractions his
theory of the "irritability of the protoplasm."[1] Haller's work
and ideas gave rise to modern experimental physiology of nerve

and muscle tissue and also to what eventually became the lie-detector. When our common language distinguishes between "the quick and the dead," it alludes to the old notion of irritability as a basic sign of life. Quick to ignite is life itself, and what's dry burns all the faster.

The trivial irritations that produce eruptions of rage are by no means trivial. Rage is like a cellular anger. It leaps up in defense of character, rejects interference, insists on maintaining our habitual way of life. "Don't tell me what to do!" "Let me do it my way!" "This is how *I* like it!" Irritability: a display of the raw urge to live. It shows the attachment of the flesh to living.

We may replace Descartes' "Cogito ergo sum" (I think, therefore I am), with "I am irritated, therefore I am." If irritability is truly a vital sign, then the grumpy old men are keeping themselves going by virtue of their instantly arousable grumpiness. The slightest provocation sets off fits of pique and leads to plots of revenge. We need our political outrage, our social prejudices, our ridiculous hatreds—not only for the content of this hostility, but for the fire.

Fury in old age is a regular phenomenon. You feel it mount when put on hold; when walking into a darkened movie theater and a pack of unknowns is blocking *your* way; when *your* parking space is taken before you can quite get to it. You hate everyone ahead of you at the counter. Who are all these people? You wish them dead.

A bad-tempered spirit is as old as civilization, a given of human nature. Neither Swift nor Mencken, neither Marx nor Dorothy Parker could have written a word without it. Many societies have gods of rage and battle; Jahweh himself was a war god given to terrifying, destructive moods, inflicting plagues, floods, and slaughter on his people with little provocation. The Greeks recognized and dramatized the anger of Hera, Athene, Aphrodite, Poseidon, Zeus, an anger embodied in the avenging Furies, who do not let sins pass and who bring a savage passion into the dramas of human lives.

Advice to seniors forgets all this. They are coddled with a mild diet of pudding and milk toast, polite condescension and soft answers. The AARP likes its elders peppy but not peppery, vigorous but not vociferous. The actual fire of emotions is denied, as if old age were merely a time of recollection in tranquillity.

Serenity keeps irritability tamed, enslaving vitality and promoting the oppressions and injustices of the status quo. Had senior citizens not joined the activists, not become MADD at drunken driving, at secondhand smoke, at unsafe cars and the devastation of dolphins, these travesties would go on and on.

Senior citizens may have retired, but they are hardly retiring—nor should they be, since they are not only senior but citizens. Their irritations can carry them to the front of the firing line, make them stand up in public meetings, lodge complaints, bring suit, fervid and fearless in defense of a cause.

Could chronic, even explosive hostility be "healthy"? Research at the Minnesota Mayo Clinic discovered that "older men tended to score on the high end of the hostility scale" compared with younger men. Yet "the older man's relative hostility level did not seem to put him at greater risk of heart disease, a result that did startle the researchers."[2]

This intensity of feeling can aid the transition to the condition of ancestor, for one of the ancestors' tasks is the sometimes violent protection of the living community. As guardian spirits, ancestors stand watch, attentive to the slightest indication that things are going wrong. Like the Furies, ancestors do not tolerate injustice. Calming meditative practices, needlepoint, basketry, and the tranquilizers offered by your caring physician all acknowledge, by trying to subdue, the irritability of the protoplasm that will "Rage, rage against the dying of the light."[3]

Anger could also indicate a desire for freedom from the long-lasting patterns of life. It is as if there is a spirit bottled up that doesn't want any longer to be caught in daily trivia, doesn't want to be in a body on this earth. Then the irritability expresses a frustration at having to be here and at waiting so long to leave. My friend Professor Malidoma Somé, an initiated elder, says that among his people in Burkina Faso the old ones are generally angry and ill-tempered, irritated by the banalities of the daily round. Part of them is already elsewhere, departed. Their irritation signifies that departure.

Whether old people are irritable because of the cellular rage to live or because they're impatient at still being here, either way, irritability belongs to late years. It will flare up spontaneously even when there are no provoking causes. And it cannot be tempered by patience, which keeps placid company side by side with the bursts of peevish annoyance.

Patience and impatience are only one set of opposing forces belonging to later years. Aging brings out all sorts of contradictions in human nature. All the complexes composing personality leap out of the basket. You become an unpredictable hydra—smiling, snapping, happy, grouchy, grumpy—all seven dwarfs. A religious believer might say this multitude of moods foreshadows another world where all is welcome and nothing can be predicted, where the lifting up to heaven is simply lifting the lid from the fullness of character, the whole jumble of unpredictable dwarfs risen in flesh, just as they are, with no apologies.

CHAPTER 12

Parting

Parting is such sweet sorrow.

Shakespeare, Romeo and Juliet

I rritability points to something more: The central control apparatus of personality is breaking down. Memory lapses are only part of this. Your feet stumble, your eyes misread, your gut belches and farts; dribbles and drips, sudden tears at unexpected kindness and just as sudden violence over an interruption; words won't come to mind. You cannot hold it together.

A mutiny is going on. The crew no longer obeys the captain. Each one starts doing its own thing in its own way. Sporadic desertions rather than a concerted mutiny; anarchy rather than revolution. Or, to shift the image, it is as if older age moves the spotlight from the ringmaster with his top hat, megaphone, and whip over to the animals and freaks in the sideshow.

The complexes come out—pettiness, querulousness, embarrassment, weepy sentimentality, envy, spite, bigotry, each in its turn shows itself, almost as if they had been put on hold, waiting for years to have their say. Many people in late years like to shock and expose; they like to make demonstrations in public, to the distress of their family, who try to hush them up and bundle them off. But once freed from central control, the partial personalities simply say, "Hi, here I am, look at me, I belong here, too." They thumb their noses at the retiring and weakened ego.

Preparation for final departure begins as coming apart. For all the social embarrassment that goes with weakened control, there is a happy reward. You feel loosened, more free. It is amazing to what extent a person who has limped for years, who wears incontinence pads, who must turn his head to hear—to say nothing of his more incapacitating deficits—is free of the constraints that we who are spared these restrictions find painful merely to contemplate. The spastic man in the wheelchair, the woman who speaks through a voice box in her throat have in some blessed way come to terms with afflictions that seem unbearable to us. We are curiously more bound because we are still imagining the condition from the ideals of our controlling ego, which they have long ago been forced to abandon and from which they have been freed.

Coming apart also frees character from personality. Personality harnesses character traits, integrates them into a self-consistent line. In old age they fall out singly, as memorable images. Distinct traits of a former husband with whom you struggled for years are released as personality dissolves. The person goes, while his careful hands stay, an image apart from his oppressive power.

These single and singular character traits live on apart from the person as a whole. We hold only parts of the dead in our memories; only characteristics remain. Ancestors are not so much composite personalities as singular traits that come to guide in particular crises. That's why there are so many angels and cherubim, so many invisible beings and blessed saints. Each carries a distinct trait and performs a specialized service.

The body, even if coming apart, even if ruined, knows what it is doing and relies upon an archetypal reason, which gives it its wisdom. Falling to pieces and coming apart find an archetypal background in the Dionysos myths.

The Greek god Dionysos was dismembered into countless pieces by persecutory enemies, the Titans. Yet he remained a figure of many guises and pursuits. He was called the

Divided/Undivided, the Loosener, the Lord of Souls, the Lord of Wild Beasts. His realm was outside the conventional constraints of the city; his dances took place on hillsides near woodlands. In the city he ruled the theater, both comic and tragic. What could be more appropriate to older age than the theatrics of comedy and tragedy!

Coming apart implicates a myth quite different from those we usually associate with strength of character. No longer Hercules, master of decisive action; no longer Artemis, ruler of animal nature, or Hera, queen of the household and upholder of family values; no longer wily dealer, communicator, and escape artist Hermes, or bright, beautiful Apollo, lover of youth.

Instead, Dionysos, Lord of Souls, the divided god who was pulled into pieces. Dionysos embodies the force of life, *zoe* (from which our "zoology"), which runs alike through all humans, animals, and plants. "Our body is Dionysian," declared the ancient writer Olympiodoros. This strange figure, even named "the stranger," was most male and most effeminate, a little child and a bearded man, wild and somber, masked and revealed, aroused and recumbent. Despite his awesome power and passion, he is usually in the company of nurses. Of all his paradoxes, perhaps the sharpest is this: This intoxicating life force, who came on the scene together with a dancing gang of prancing satyrs and raving devotees, was also declared to be one and the same as Hades, invisible god of the souls in the underworld.

When we translate these images of myth into the psychology of aging, can we not recognize ourselves in the mirror of Dionysos and in the mysterious happenings told of his cult? Don't we old ones also metaphorically exhibit the traits of being childish, though bearded; wild, yet needy of nursing; sexy, and yet impotent; boisterously male, and soft-breastedly female? Aren't we also sometimes as confused as a drunk? Don't we find kinship as we age with our plants and animal pets? And aren't we, too, misperceived as freakish—as a comedy and tragedy both? If we see only the symptoms and name them psychiatrically, we miss the method in the madness, the myth in the mess.

Still, why the coming apart? Why is breaking down into pieces part of departing? Dionysos, again, may help us to understand. His dynamic intensity was thought to be distributed like sparks of intelligence through all matter, like hidden bits of information that are also an interior vivification. In a Dionysian world, everything is alive, even the dead. In our late years most of the people we know, who come to us in dream and memory, are dead, and yet they feel vividly alive. We are moved most strongly by images of dead friends, dead loves, dead family, images that remain poignantly vital even if, or because, they are dead.

———

We come apart to leave, and also to join. Over the grave, the Christian minister speaks Dionysian metaphors. "She is gathered to her ancestors"; "He unites with his loved ones"; "the community of the departed." Perhaps it's not our whole self that resurrects, but merely certain unique characteristics that must separate out from the whole. Then, falling apart opens the way to a new reassembling. Here is the myth of Dionysos, the Divided/Undivided.

A hidden intelligence lies within each of our body parts. Thousands of years ago, in the high culture of Egypt, the body was taken apart before mummification; several different organs were placed in jars, each with a particular animal head, suggesting that each belonged to a specific god and was infused with its intelligence. For us, it is rare to find intelligence in our bones and organs. We hardly know we consist of body parts until they break down.

We train ourselves to sense our body parts by undergoing bodywork or physiotherapy, doing hatha yoga or dance exercises, or by working out on steel machines. Mostly, we discover body parts—the kidney and the knee, say—when something goes wrong with them. Then the knee becomes a focus of concentrated attention, its angles and tensions fascinating; the kidney becomes a study of its own. The part speaks to you as a discrete phenomenon and is treated by a distinct medical specialty. Rehabilitation after a stroke or an injury affords a similar awareness, as it reintegrates misfunctioning parts into the undivided whole. It is this kind of awareness that Dionysos brings, the intimate knowledge of parts that otherwise function flawlessly in silence, dumb.

I am, of course, not recommending kidney stones and twisted knees. Suffering is no virtue, nor is it necessarily a path to virtue. Suffering can make us as calcified and twisted as the kidney and knee that brought it on. I am suggesting, however, that the body is a kind of temple (as Greeks and Christians both have frequently said), in which the gods can make their home. It is both a literal structure for medical science and a poetic architecture for psychological insight. When troubles take over the body, its afflictions may be indicating not only what is wrong medically, but what can be learned psychologically from what is wrong. In that case, what is wrong remains just as wrong but becomes, as well, a surprising source of intelligence and even vitality.

Perhaps we must come apart in order to depart so that we can appreciate what has been carrying us along for so many years—those faithful kidneys, those stalwart joints, giving uncomplaining service. Before the body becomes a corpse in a casket it seems to have a lot to say to the soul. It begins to act up, break down, and speak out. Like a plant we tend, or an animal, the part lets us know what it likes and how it can best be favored: with which teas, which temperatures, which poultices and positions. This is some of the wisdom imparted to the elderly departing. This is the information we look for from healing old women, from *curanderos* and *stregas* and shamans. This is what can make the elderly useful as elders to others' troubles. Where do they get their intelligence and vitality from, and their unique characters? From their troubles, their breakdowns. It is not that they use alternative medicine, but that they "belong" to an alternative God, Dionysos, who had himself been torn apart and whose paradoxical freakishness made him the eternal alternative to the mighty Olympians.

CHAPTER 13

Erotics

Of all problems eroticism is the most mysterious,
the most general and the least straightforward.
For the [person] . . . whose life is open to exuberance,
eroticism is the greatest problem of all.

Georges Bataille

Eh, mister! Your fly is open, mister.

James Joyce

According to a tradition that goes back to the *Problemata* attributed to Aristotle, old age is the period of life when lust becomes most extravagant. The old are under the influence of Saturn and therefore succumb easily to the *furor melancholicus,* a condition of the psyche that fosters creative art, prophecy, and exaggerated emotional instability. Other terms used for this visionary possession are "excess of pneuma" (too much airy spirit) and "heightening of the *vis imaginativa*" (force of imagination). As physical powers wane, imagination cuts loose and runs wild. On the one hand, impotence, misogyny, and depressive isolation; on the other, the lewd fantasies of the dirty old man, that old goat.

"Melancholics" were susceptible "especially to visual images."[1] "Mental pictures or images (*phantasmata*) affected the mind [of the melancholic] more strongly and were more compelling than was the case with other people." "This exaggerated irritability of the imagining power (*vis imaginativa*) was later believed . . . to enhance the power of visual imagination."[2] According to this Aristotelian physiology, "all really outstanding men, whether in the realm of the arts or in those of poetry, philosophy or statesmanship—even Socrates and Plato—, were melancholics."[3]

The ancient physiology explains quite rationally why airy fantasies (*phantasmata*) literally affect the genitals: "For the sexual act is connected with the generation of air, as is shown by the fact that the virile organ quickly increases from a small size by inflation."[4] Lustful thoughts and images swell the organs.

Leonardo da Vinci at the beginnings of modern scientific experimentation graphically demonstrated this ancient pneumatic physiology. His cross-sectional drawings of the penis (based on anatomical dissection) showed *two* passages, one for seminal fluids, the other for the pneuma or *aura seminalis*.[5] Erection required imagination.

Today's physiology tells a different story. It leaves out the heightened *vis imaginativa,* reporting only that "the ovaries in women and the sexual capacity of men decline faster than perhaps anything else in the body."[6] As female lubrication dries and male erection withers, performance anxiety increases, thereby increasing performance failure, thereby increasing performance anxiety, ad infinitum. The comic tragedy of old bodies trying to get it on.

While performance subsides, the range of erotic fantasy extends and enlivens. Samuel Atkin, psychoanalyst, afflicted with Parkinson's, reports in his faithfully honest diary:

Dec. 1st . . . Awoke in a state of sexual excitement. Hurray! The erotic impulse still operates. Although my Parkinsonian exhaustion leaves me weak, a barely audible voice, dizzy, practically unable to move or to write, in pain, I feel "zestful." I am having a good time. Here is victory over decay. . . . New antics. This erotic upsurge. A creative impulse. Pratfalls. A clown. (The *tragic* clown.)

Feb 10th—I started my day in a depressed state—half dead. I will end it in glory. Erotic thoughts: I possess three things—(1) an active mind, perhaps less capable of dealing with the tasks of mature living, but fully capable of erotic fantasies; (2) a phallus that has lost its full virility and ejaculatory capability, but is still capable of pleasurable feelings, *thanks to erotic imagination*; (3) my woman . . . object of my romantic feelings . . . [italics mine].[7]

Dr. Atkin made these notes at age eighty-eight. In Pablo Picasso's eighty-seventh year, between March 16 and October 5, 1968, he completed 347 graphically erotic engravings. These masterpieces are concrete depictions of genitals, of gazing voyeurs, of voluptuaries, of sexual intercourse, and yet they are distanced by means of distortions and by a parade of intercessionary figures—costumed representatives of the artistic past, pimps and bordello couplers, musicians—and by mirrors, masks, models. The blatant pelvic spread of pornography is transformed by the imaginative context in which the lewd exposure is placed; body transposed into imagination, sexuality into erotica.

The balance struck between the salacious and the sardonic makes the engravings at once fresh, naïve, grotesque, bittersweet, touching—and self-mocking. The concrete genitals become decorative, fantastic, ridiculous.

"I feel zestful," says Dr. Atkin. "Thanks to erotic imagination. . . . Here is victory over decay. . . . This erotic upsurge. A creative impulse." Two octogenarians on the same track. What but the erotic imagination gave Picasso the zest and stamina to turn out some fifty finished pieces a month, seven months straight? "The old myth that sexual aging leads to general aging has a germ of truth."[8] Dr. Atkin and Señor Picasso prove this in reverse. Perhaps the erotic imagination can do more for physical and intellectual vigor in old age than all the barbells and lap pools put together. We do not live zestfully on bone and muscle alone; something else, the erotic, must fire the spirit.

Why must lust still compel the aged character? Why, for that matter, sexual fantasy at all, in anyone, if not to further vital delight—of which procreative utility is only an occasional side effect? A simple verse by William Butler Yeats states the case:

> You think it horrible that lust and rage
> Should dance attention upon my old age;
> They were not such a plague when I was young;
> What else have I to spur me into song?[9]

In a letter to a friend and former lover, Yeats at age sixty-seven wrote, "I shall be a sinful man to the end, and think upon my death-bed of all the nights I wasted in my youth." The next year, aged sixty-eight, he wrote another friend: "The man who ignores the poetry of sex . . . finds the bare facts written up on the walls of a privy, or is himself compelled to write them there."[10]

All the while, as Yeats recognized the compelling power of sexual fantasy, he bemoaned his physical decrepitude:

> Consume my heart away; sick with desire
> And fastened to a dying animal . . .

And

> What shall I do with this absurdity—
> O heart, O troubled heart—this caricature,
> Decrepit age that has been tied to me
> As to a dog's tail?
>
> Never had I a more
> Excited, passionate, fantastical
> Imagination, nor an ear and eye
> That more expected the impossible—

Decrepit age and heightened fantasy appear together, and belong together. They are co-relatives, requiring each other. Even more, Yeats declares that "bodily decrepitude is wisdom," the wisdom of the "passionate, fantastical imagination" that accompanies the decrepitude.[11]

For Walt Whitman, erotics was the key to imaginative freedom. "Of physiology from top to toe I sing . . . of Life immense in passion, pulse, and power."[12] Near his end in 1891, Whitman continued to imagine what Yeats calls the "poetry of sex." While designing and supervising the construction of his mausoleum, he was also engaged in publishing the tenth revision—what he called the "Deathbed edition"—of *Leaves of Grass,* that "dirty book" for which he had been summarily fired from his job at the Department of Interior some twenty-five years earlier.

During his last months Whitman wrote letters, notes, and many poems, parallel with increasingly extreme bodily decay. The autopsy revealed tubercular abscesses under the sternum and in the left foot; tuberculosis-ravaged lungs, intestines, and liver; bad kidneys and a suprarenal cyst; an enlarged prostate and an enormous bladder stone; brain atrophy; and arteriosclerosis.[13] Whitman's perspicacity was as extraordinary as his decay: There was no deathbed confession, no compulsion to tell all on the privy wall. As a patron saint of the naked body, masturbation, and sexual love between men, Whitman nonetheless made clear the distinction between behavior and imagination. What he did was private business; what he imagined was there to be read.

When pressed, during his last year, to come forward and state his position on male erotics, he replied: *"restraint . . .* I at certain moments let the spirit impulse (demon) rage its utmost, its wildest, damndest—(I feel to do so in my *L of G* and I do so)." Restraint provides the occasion for Yeats's "excited, passionate, fantastical Imagination." Whitman explained the tie between personal restraint and imaginative freedom in a note:

> We arrange our lives with reference to what society conventionally rules and makes right. We retire to our rooms for freedom; to undress, bathe, unloose everything in freedom. These, and much else, would not be proper in society. . . . [T]he soul of a man or woman demands, enjoys compensation in the highest directions for this very restraint of himself or herself, level'd to the average, or rather mean, low. . . . To balance this indispensable abnegation, the free minds of poets relieve themselves, and strengthen and enrich mankind with free flights in all the directions not tolerated by ordinary society.[14]

If imaginative freedom "in all the directions" requires compliance with societal average, the reverse is also true. The restraints imposed both by ordinary society's mores and by aging physiology require imaginative freedom, which, according to Whitman, strengthens and enriches the very society that finds it intolerable. In old age, erotic fantasy is more than a symptom, more than a compensation. It becomes a private necessity and, consequently, a societal benefit.

———

Male fantasy is said to be more concrete and organ focused, female more imprecise and encompassing—witness romantic novels; nonetheless, the *intensity* of fantasy is shared equally. If a very old woman is visited by memories of kisses under summer trees and a very old man by the recollection of a slippery vagina in the back room of a Tijuana bar, both remembrances are images; both exemplify the ageless, genderless erotic imagination.

Genderless? Yes—and no. The usual analysis of erotic life divides people in terms of physiological gender and cultural roles. But neither character nor imagination is gender-determined; consequently, neither is eroticism. Erotic differences depend largely on cultural background, economic level, education, religion, family, and peers—along with genetic inheritance. There are hyperactive women and supinely passive men; women ashamed of their lasciviousness and men ashamed of their indifference, ashamed because the dogmas of gender have told them how they ought to be. Sexual life is primarily imaginative life; it starts there, feeds there, and persists there long after the abrupt and sometimes absurd actualities of the events themselves. And gender is not the determinant of imagination.

The French actress Jeanne Moreau chose roles and directed films that allowed her to "grow old disgracefully." At sixty-four, she played "an exotic flame-haired free spirit," who, in order to save a young girl from a disastrous marriage, intervenes by "sexually straddling the groom." Her career, and the recognition of her abilities, increased in late years, together with her provocative eroticism. "When you speak of sexuality," Moreau said, "most people expect physical sex, but sexuality starts in the mind with imagination."

Alice Neel, one of America's best painters of the twentieth century, said she loved "that filthy character" Jean Genet. "Do you know . . . because everything that happened he turned into literature. It couldn't be too base for him."

Beatrice Wood, a ceramist who lived to be 105, continued, even after age eighty-five, to play "the courtesan, flirting with outrageous coquettishness." "She loved to cultivate the myth of her wickedness and rampant sensuality." Again, "cultivating the myth" is what counts, as, for instance, Anaïs Nin and May Sarton also demonstrate. They claimed they had, or imagined they had, lover after lover. Erotic fantasy and endless writing went side by side until the end of their long lives. "To May at seventy, the loved one had virtually been reduced to a shot of speed in the poetic vein." She referred to women lovers as "muses."

Essential to the art of Colette and Marguerite Duras as they aged was the beauty incarnated in their young lovers. Colette at fifty took as a lover her former husband's son, aged twenty. Duras's Yann was twenty-five.

The presence of beauty in a young body as an inspiration for the old is a theme analyzed already by Plato (*Symposium*). Did the presence of ever-fresh dancing bodies provide Martha Graham with muses for ever-inventive choreographies into her nineties? Did the magnificent tribespeople of the Nuba region of the Sudan do something similar for Leni Riefenstahl, who filmed them in her seventies?

Isak Dinesen and Georgia O'Keeffe were each accompanied and attended by much younger men, themselves artists, who spurred their imagination in old age. As O'Keeffe's eyesight was failing, an artist, Hamilton, became her project. The younger poet Thorkild Bjornvig entered into a mystical literary pact with Dinesen, who was then sixty-three, that raised their imaginations to a fever pitch of inspiration. Evenings "were spent drinking wine, quoting poetry to each other, playing Schubert . . . making imaginary voyages and taking imaginary lovers." Some years later, Dinesen again passed an evening with her younger poet and told him a story, in the genre of "confessing one's worst sin," of seducing a cabin boy years and years earlier, when she knew she had syphilis. Whether this was "pure invention" or literal fact, it demonstrates how the imagination returns in later years to lasting images of arousal.[15]

———

All too often, conventional wisdom convinces the aging to fear the shameless images that come uncontrollably to their minds. Seniors need, rather, to hear that there is reason in these sexualized fantasies, which connect eroticism with spirit and imaginative power. The *vis imaginativa* that joins sex and inspiration finds its symbol in "the typically Greek invention of the phallos-bird," which can be an "agent of travel in strange realms and may substitute for more normal angels," writes classicist Emily Vermeule.[16]

Sexualized fantasy can overleap the upright picket fences of convention, which finds it intolerable that old people, especially women, are still libidinal. William James, a good New Englander and the most eminent of all American psychologists, wrote about the "fantastic and unnecessary character of human wants." James says of these "wants" that "even when their gratification seems farthest off, the uneasiness they occasion is still the best guide of his life, and will lead him to issues entirely beyond his present powers of reckoning. Prune down his extravagance, sober him, and you undo him."[17]

Many sorts of images, written, painted, modeled in clay, projected on the television glass, evoke a voyeuristic response. We find it hard to turn away because we are subliminally turned on. Images arouse. The viewer is drawn in, and instantly two dragon guardians appear, Fear and Shame, who box us into the conventions called normal. The "fear of arousal," writes Columbia art historian David Freedberg, lies at the root of censorship, iconoclasm, and the resistance to imagination. The twin beasts we must overcome when engaged by our private images are not lust and longing but fear and shame. Why should I be so conflicted about the extravagances of imagination? After all, they are "merely" images. Why should I be ashamed?

To serve as an ancestor in a culture is to have overcome some of its shames and fears. To be a mentor to generations younger than yours is to know their obsessions and yet be freer of them.

Some freedom can come from realizing you are not solely to blame for the conflict brought on by arousal. The source lies deeper than human nature. It is archetypal, a conflict among the gods. The call of Dionysos tends to upset the normal course of civilization, whose wise overseer Athene did not permit his goat in her terrain. Dionysos, "Lord of Women," called to both genders and all ages to join his rituals. Women left their household duties to follow him into the hills for release and raving. Two "old-timers" with gray hair in Euripides' play *The Bacchae* go off to dance with Dionysos "all night and all day." It is hard to accept in doddering, impotent, but fantasy-full late years that you somehow belong more to Dionysos than you ever did in your youth, when you thought of yourself as a hotshot of indefatigable appetite.

Old people are perhaps explorers, after all. Since their capacity for sexual behavior is limited, they need not fear or censor arousal. They can allow themselves to be taken to the farthest undiscovered reaches. The absurdity of old desire is not shameful but rather belongs to the wisdom of their foolishness. As subjects of ridicule—of the countless jokes about sex in the old-age home, sex of the old man with a younger wife, old couples' sex therapy—only the old can bring out the ridiculousness of sexuality. The young try too hard; they are too engrossed, too literal, or too in love.

Erotics thus moves from the great love to the big laugh. From the beginning of theater under the patronage of Dionysos, the audience watched the follies of old sex. The comic interludes that played alongside the Greek tragedies were marked by verbal obscenities, gnarled, ridiculous men, and lascivious satyrs.

Central to the mystery initiations of women at Eleusis in Greece was the telling of a transformative, even redemptive tale. Demeter, goddess of grain and the earth's fecundity, sat on a "laughless rock," immobile, veiled, and grieving the rape of her daughter. No power could move her from desolation. Then an old woman, Baubo ("Belly"), performed an obscene dance and exposed her genitals.¹⁸ Demeter laughed, restoring the fertility on which the well-being of all the world depended.¹⁹

Other mythical figures also come into play, especially Aphrodite whom the Spartans called *ambologera,* "she who holds off old age." An Aphrodite temple in Corinth was dedicated to Peeping Aphrodite, a hint that even prurient voyeurism has a mythical counterpart.²⁰ Aphrodite was also called *porneia,* and in that capacity menaced the aged monks in their ascetic desert retreats with tempting visitations.²¹ We do not have to be monks to retreat to asceticism or live in the desert of dried-up fantasies. Simply by renouncing the erotic imagination and believing it inappropriate to later years, we join their company.

How trapped we are, how inadequate are our times for making sense of our sensuality! Lust in late years has a hard time finding justification. It demands an imaginative perspective. Otherwise, we believe the only impotence is literal, physical, and expect Medicare to provide Viagra. But the enfeebled and lustless *imagination* may be far more indicative of decline of powers. The ancient physiology insisted that potency depended on the spirit's fantasy, and the new physiology of sildenafil (Viagra) reformulates the same priority of spirit over matter: "Sildenafil produces an erection only when the man is sexually aroused."²² Imagination precedes performance; performance depends only secondarily on Viagra.

The sexualization of the old mind is part of its unusual wisdom. It shows a character that no longer separates pleasure from virtue. It places no restrictions on imaginative freedom. It presents character strengthened by imagining rather than by stiff-lipped willpower. The strength of this character lies less in controlling its lustful fantasies than in understanding their transpersonal nature as a cosmic dynamic.²³ As imagination shapes the world with images, so it flows through the human psyche, whose primary data are images. "The psyche consists essentially of images," said Jung; "Image *is* psyche," and "The psyche creates reality every day. The only expression I can use for this activity is *fantasy.*"²⁴ Whether imagination is a creature of the brain, or given by God as a counterpart to his creativity, or the work of demonic and illusory lower powers, or a reflection of the soul's aesthetic need—these are philosophical choices. It is not the control and eradication of images that makes for virtue, but their ordering. The ordering of images, their expression and elaboration, was always a function of myth and a province of the arts. That is why artists preside over this chapter.

CHAPTER 14

Anesthesia

An aged man is but a paltry thing,
A tattered coat upon a stick . . .

W. B. Yeats

That our senses lose their acuity in later years needs special comment since this anesthesia of the old is so much taken for granted. Going deaf or dim-sighted, being unable to smell that your clothes need cleaning or to fully taste your food, all this we expect. We leave the world blandly, or so it is supposed.

Let me repeat: What is going on in the body is trapped in the mind's idea of the body. All the while we are losing acuity, we are intensifying Yeats's "fantastical eye." We can spin out from one wild strawberry a whole northern summer, from one tasty tea cake a vast French novel. The sensuous acuity remains, but has become detached from the senses. It is now more literary and less literal. Sensation has fled from the adolescent coming home, grabbing a a half-gallon of cold milk and gulping it down from the carton. Now it takes very little milk to release buckets of accumulated recollections, all the spilled milk and milk of human kindness that give delight to the mental palate. My cup runneth over—because it is a smaller cup.

Besides the release from Gargantua and his demanding appetites, anesthesia brings another benefit: You no longer register pain as vividly as you did as a child. Good thing, too, since in late years there are often a lot of probing procedures to undergo. The burns and cuts and dental work hurt less, even if you fuss more. Freud didn't fuss, and as he aged he went through more than thirty dreadful operations on his jaw and palate at a time when anesthesia was crude at best. I find Freud's biography more relevant to aging than much of his theory.

I must admit here to doubting the hypothesis that aging weakens our senses. Is there truly a loss of sensual acuity in later years? Major figures of tea tasting, wine selection, and perfume blending, as well as great chefs and tobacconists, reach their prime as they age. Aged conductors of symphony orchestras, master painters, fashion designers who must distinguish the tiniest differences in weaves and hues and finish—are they all half deaf and going blind? Do they not perceive *better* than in earlier years?

Can the ability to fine-tune the senses be sufficiently measured in terms of olfactory receptors, trigeminal nerve endings, and taste buds. Does the subtlety of the connoisseur not also depend on a subtle body that notices finely, as if spirit judged spirit, as if perception in older age precedes sensation, reversing the laws of mechanistic psychology? Might the expert's fine eye perceive beyond the retina's capacity, and the ear notice what the dulled drum doesn't?

Research into taste sensations reports that "taste sensitivity and perception actually change little in most healthy older people. When taste sensitivity does decrease, it may be linked to memory loss and changes in perception of tastes, rather than to changes in taste buds."[1] Since imagination affects memory and perception, what distinguishes old taste connoisseurs from other seniors dependent on taste enhancers may be not the quantity of their taste buds but their still freshly budding imagining powers.

Let me go back to Heraclitus once more. He said that souls in the underworld perceive by smell. That is, the deeper psyche "beneath" the daily world uses other modes of sensing. And, Heraclitus said, "if all things became smoke [that is, lose their materiality and the materialist way of regarding them], the nostrils would distinguish them."

This arcane observation deserves our attention. Heraclitus'

ideas remain fertile even after two and a half millennia as they have composted into the subsoil of most later psychological thinking. For contemporary psychology, this statement asserts that the underworld infuses the soul with a different aesthetic capacity. If so, the task in later years, as physical limits increase, becomes an exercise in taste. So often these late years show increasing anesthesia, by which I mean aesthetic decline—careless dressing, cheapened color choices, coarsened sensations. The decline to shopping-mall and fast-food aesthetics is not entirely due to economic and psychological depression or to the prescription drugs we take to numb us down. Tastelessness derives also from the neglect of the deeper soul, which has aesthetic needs, apart from physical satisfaction. The soul shrivels without images and sensations of beauty.

Heraclitus further implies two systems of perception, perhaps two perceiving bodies. One is the aging physiological system; the other, the psychological inhabitant of that system, who may be fine-tuning—intuitively picking up the scent of things—even as the first declines. To recognize the possibility of a sophisticated aesthetic in older age, we need to discover more sophisticated *ideas* about taste and the senses in relation to the soul.

Although our physical body, which receives the world's sensations, has already begun to let go, the subtle body that perceives the world's beauty and ugliness hasn't quit.

Robert Butler, the eminent researcher of old age, makes this telling point about heightened aesthetics in last years: "The elemental things in life—children, plants, nature, human touching (physical and emotional), color, shape—may assume greater significance as people sort out the more important from the less important."[2] Importance does not result from sensation only, or from simplicity. If it did, we would still prefer sugary childhood candies and the salty goo of fast-food pizza to the subtleties concocted by multistarred chefs. "Importance," which Alfred North Whitehead placed among the first principles for understanding all human endeavors, governs our choices among values. "Importance is derived from the immanence of infinitude in the finite."[3] A sixth sense leads the other five and is immanent within them. Values of infinitude enhance the sensate world. It is this transcendence that connoisseurs of the senses seek in their tastings, smellings, and listenings. Taste can grow with aging as the values of the invisible and the visible oscillate less widely, interpenetrate more closely.

If importance grows as leaving the world nears, then we might expect the aged to be expert witness to aesthetic sensitivity. Not that everyone on a deathbed becomes Matisse, afflicted yet exquisitely productive, or De Kooning, whose mind was lost to Alzheimer's while his "subtle body" went on painting extraordinary works. But if we forget this sensitivity in the old, noticing only the stale smells and habitually rumpled disorder, we who visit them are culpable of physical abuse. That is, we abuse them by reducing them to their physical facts. Why not meet them at their best?

———

In Japan, poets and monks on the verge of death compose—supposedly as their very last act—a *jisei,* a brief farewell poem to life. In 1841, the great poet Daibai wrote, at age seventy:

> My seventy years—a withered
> pampas tail and all around it
> iris blooming.

Saruo (1923, age sixty-five) wrote:

> Cherry blossoms fall
> on a half-eaten
> dumpling.

These following two come from two different haiku poets both called Seiju.
Seiju (1776, age seventy-five):

> Not even for a moment
> do things stand still—witness
> color in the trees.

Seiju (1779, age eighty-six):

> Water veins
> stain rice fields different
> shades of green.[4]

In each of these examples the poet serves as an appreciative witness to the blooming iris, the shades of green, the color in the trees. The elemental things in life assume a greater significance. . . .

Rather like a Japanese *jisei* is this autumn poem, written in a nursing home by Nadya Catalfano, ninety-four:

> Your leaves sound different
> I couldn't understand why
> The leaves at that time of year
> Had a rustle about them
> And they would drop
> At the least little thing
> And I would listen
> And pick up some of them.[5]

Or, in the words of Yeats:

> An aged man is but a paltry thing,
> A tattered coat upon a stick, unless
> Soul clap its hands and sing, and louder sing
> For every tatter in its mortal dress. . . .[6]

What matters is what we do with the tatters and shards. Daibai, at seventy, speaks of the iris; Nadya Catalfano, at ninety-four, listens to falling leaves; Saruo, at sixty-three, observes his exquisite dumpling, so much left untasted.

Perception continues in the mind's eye. What we no longer see, we see in another light. Dulled, inaccurate, inconstant our senses may be, yet the imagination still can sing, and louder.

CHAPTER 15

Heart Failure

See this heart of mine,
it weeps for itself and pleads for mercy.
The Egyptian Book of the Dead

Valve dysfunction. Electrical arrhythmia. Aortic aneurysm. Arterial constriction. Ventricular congestion. Hammering high pressure. Deposits of fatty plaque. The pump is wearing down; pipings clogged, stiffened; the walls thinning and the muscle tired. Clinical language whispers warnings and accompanies each sudden exertion. Recollections of Grandmother on the floor, of Father gasping—their massive coronaries. The heart skips a beat; an indigestion cramp—is this *it*? Heart failure haunts later years.

Could these recurrent fears of acute heart failure reflect other, more chronic failures of the heart? Could heart troubles in later years also refer to a troubled heart? No doubt, somewhere along the way each heart has failed. To medicalize these painful seizures into failures of the bag of blood inside your rib cage constricts the heart's rich implications. There are more hearts than the one that shows up in clinical imaging.

The clinical heart was first put into language by William Harvey, a British physician of the seventeenth century who brilliantly tracked the circulation and calculated the volume of the blood, and who was the first to articulate the nature of the clinical heart. Hold the heart in your hands, Harvey says:

It may be felt to become harder during its action. This hard-
ness proceeds from tension, just as when the forearm is
grasped, its muscles . . . become tense and firm when [these
muscles] move the fingers. . . . during action the heart . . . becomes erect, hard and smaller.[1]

Erect, hard, small, tense, "the original and foundation from
which all power is derived"—here begins the modern heart and
its power to attack. Displaced from within, it becomes a miraculous pump given over to human hands for measurements
and operations. Open-heart surgery and heart replacements
follow logically from Harvey's writings. This is the heart whose
attacks we fear, the ticker we jog to keep running, the power
source we would prolong by tranquilizing passionate intensity.
("Take it easy. Keep calm. Stay cool.") The only permissible excess is extensive exercise good for the heart.

Can metaphor determine fact? A research cardiologist,
Emile R. Mohler, presented findings of bony growths in heart
valves that cannot be accounted for by simple calcium accumulations. "It's startling that cellular organization is involved,"
Mohler says. "It's bizarre." He suggests that the bony formations in the heart valves "may form when stresses in a valve at-
tract roving immune cells."[2]

The hardened heart that is needed to meet competitive stress
has become so literal a foundation of our daily reality that we
are fast losing other ideas of "heart," which reigned before Harvey and still affect our feelings and our language. Character
used to be spoken of in terms of the "heart" of courage, or the
"heart" of generosity and loyalty. This heart heartens the down-
trodden, cooks a hearty meal, and has a hearty laugh. It has
heart for the fight and beats for what's right: family, friends,
comrades, causes.

The second heart is even more familiar—the Valentine heart
of love. We give our heart away, cry our heart out, let the heart
break, are left heartsick each time a song, a scene, a keepsake
floats back.

A third heart was best described by great early Christian

writers, especially St. Augustine (354–430 C.E.). This is the heart of subjective feeling, the inmost person, one's true character. It is "mine," even *me:* "where I am, whatever I am."[3] Augustine equates the heart with *intima mea* and writes of it as an "inward dwelling," a "shared bedroom," a "closet" of intimacy. Because the heart is so deep and so private, Augustine often refers to it as an "abyss" and asks, Can one ever truly know this heart, in oneself or in another? "Whose heart is seen into? What one is engaged with, what one is inwardly capable of, inwardly purposing, wishing . . . who shall comprehend?"[4]

Christian writers also elaborated on the Sacred Heart of compassion. They established devotional practices to open the heart's closet to the suffering of the world. The Sacred Heart is the heart of compassionate mysticism; it sets out a discipline of love parallel with the path of the heart in Hinduism (Bhakti yoga) and the mothering, discriminating intelligence of the heart (*Binah*) in Kabbalist meditations. Contemplation of the Sacred Heart leads one beyond personal subjective feeling, expanding character toward charity, pity, and mercy.

The oldest heart of all appears in ancient Egyptian myths: the heart of Ptah, who created the world from the imagination of his heart. Everything around us, and we too, originate in the heart of Ptah and take form by virtue of his speech. The New Testament—"In the beginning was the Word, and the Word was with God"—states the same idea, except that for ancient Egypt the words start from the heart and express its imaginative power. The world was first imagined, then declared.

Imagination, the ability to see things as images, is an ability of the heart, according to the influential Islamic philosophy of Ibn Arabi (d. 1240).[5] All the figures haunting our imagination, that invisible population of angels and daimones, ghosts and ancestors with whom we sleep at night, with whom we talk in reverie, become vividly real only to the awakened heart. Otherwise we assume them to be inventions, projections, and fantasies.

This imagining heart converts such indefinables as soul, depth, beauty, dignity, love—as well as character and the idea of "heart" itself—into felt actualities, the very essence of life. Without this heart, the cavity in our chest has only Harvey's pump to keep us going.

All these different hearts continue to thrive in daily life—we still put a hand on our breast when confessing our truest convictions, as if our words were coming straight from the Augustinian private depths. We still write, on the card sent with the roses, "I love you with all my heart."

Character is concerned with the heart failures of love, inner truth, and honor, and with the suppression of beauty. For it is a daily fact that we tend to keep beauty out of our lives lest it strike our hearts and kindle fierce longings we do not know how to appease. An ECG will not reveal anything about these weaknesses, nor can a stress test expose them. Times when courage failed, when we held back our cordiality, lacked pity, or betrayed our heart's calling can preoccupy later years as much as any lab findings. Heart disease and heart unease may be as near each other in fact as in language.

I am not suggesting simplistic conversions of body into mind, such as "Clogged arteries are really blocked passions," or "Panicky arrythmias are cowardly avoidances," as if expressive psychotherapy could prevent a myocardial infarction. I do mean, however, that character demands attention to core essentials, which require other sorts of discipline than giving up smoking and cutting out butter. Life review in an armchair can be an exhausting exercise of imagining, stretching the heart-core of character at least as far as a brisk walk with the dog.

I have never forgotten one encounter with a woman in the Zurich city asylum where I did some of my clinical training. She gave me one of my first lessons about the vital necessity of imagination. At issue was her heart.

She sat in a wheelchair because she was elderly and feeble. She told the psychiatrist interviewing her that she was dead because she had lost her heart. He asked her to place her hand on her breast to feel her heart beating: It must still be there, if she could feel it beat. "That," she said, "is not my real heart." They looked at each other. We apprentices looked on. Nothing more was said.

Since the idea of character relies more upon the heart than upon any other body part, fears of succumbing to a heart attack may also indicate fears of submitting to attacks of character. Perhaps it is not only the attrition caused by life's stresses that hardens the heart, but failed contrition for our heart's smallness. And contrition definitely belongs to later years.

Younger people and those swimming upstream and caught in midlife currents often worry too much over their wrongdoings. Younger people must live life forward, ahead of their scruples and toward their ideals. They risk an overdose of therapeutic introspection. Strictures of guilt in younger years reinforce the internalized correctional institutions that impose conformity, robbing youth of its experimental liberty and oppressing middle years with even more responsibility. Besides, youthful guilt robs age of one of its final bitter pleasures: contrition.

"Contrition: the condition of being distressed in mind for some fault or injury done," says the *Oxford English Dictionary*. The old verb "contrite" means "bruise, crush, abrade." The heart crushed by its own faults is suffering another kind of massive coronary event that brings deep pain.

Small pain, too, like the prick of conscience, the abrasive pebble in the shoe. The aged philosopher Santayana, whom I visited in Rome as a brazen and callow young man, said that he had once, on returning to Spain after living in England for years, confused the coins of the two countries when tipping a waiter. The waiter stared at the tip; Santayana stared down the waiter for his impudence. Only when it was too late to make amends did Santayana realize his mistake and how paltry his tip had been. "Do you know," said the philosopher, then well over eighty, "this bothers me yet."

As you lie rigid in your bed or stare out over water, the heart reenacts how you betrayed your friend forty years ago, played the evil sister, the negligent daughter, the shirking friend. You see clearly and feel fully the injuries caused to spouses, parents, lovers, partners, dependents strewn in the wake of your self-centered demands and delusional beliefs. Of all these injuries, those done to your own calling through failure to respond with passion to the heart's imagination hurt most. With its relentless attacks, contrition exposes the heart's failures.

Since guilt is retrospective and recognizes no statute of limitations, it can always dredge up more faults, accusing us of what we did and declaring what we should have done. Too late. The past has passed away, the injured parties are long gone, reconciliation is out of range. Contrition redeems no faults. It is wholly an inward act, relieving guilt to the past by reliving guilt for the past, an appeasement of ghosts. It is not the past that is tempered by contrition, but the gnawing guilt about it.

Why must the aged heart be taxed with such heavy work? Why not let the past rest in peace? But it is character that cannot rest in peace.

Ancient Egyptian texts describing the preparations for life beyond show images of the heart as a scale balanced against a feather. Contrition lightens the heart, clearing it of dross. The Egyptians evidently thought that faults and injuries weigh the heart down. Unresolved guilts make us look backward, the wrong direction for leaving. In bed at night, or at the water's edge, we are filtering the residues accumulated by more than three billion heartbeats.

Contrition lifts from the heart the weight of the dead past, making mercy possible. "O my heart, my mother; my heart, my mother! My heart of my existence upon earth. May naught stand up to oppose me in Judgement," says the Egyptian *Book of the Dead*. Your image, encrusted with history, frees itself from that history; your native being is restored not to harmless innocence or bland amnesia, but to the essential lines of your bruised and faulty structure, you as you are, unable to be otherwise. Your character.

CHAPTER 16

Return

Go directly to Jail. Do not pass Go.
Do not collect $200.

L ong gone the prom and its exhilarating agonies; the faded
yearbook photos. Yet it takes only one small fall and, like
the crew of the Starship *Enterprise,* we dissolve to be beamed up
into another landscape: high school. There is a calling to return
to that time when the heart opened so utterly, a call so strong
that in late life a failed date of half a century earlier becomes a
sudden successful reunion, a marriage. Widows and widowers
in their seventies find each other again as the girls and boys they
cannot help but be. A piece of everyone's soul is imprisoned in
high school, serving a life sentence without parole, no matter
how good her or his behavior since then as mother, as father, as
citizen and taxpayer, as patient on the analyst's couch.

A recent statistic revealed that one third of all adult males in
the United States, and one quarter of all adult women would
choose to stay *permanently* at the ages between fifteen and nineteen: a life sentence to high school.

Is it high school? Is that what the soul wants, or does it long
for something that fifteen to nineteen represents? Is it merely
boosted testosterone and wet dreams, driving the first car, the
first hit, dating, dancing, the gang, the guys, the kids in the old
crowd, the defiant escapades, your music, our song? The soul

longs for the torment of early beauty, for which high school is a stand-in.

As mature parents in midlife we were amazed by the vapid silliness of teenagers and their pretentious sincerity, and we groaned over the excruciating awkwardness that marked our own high school days. In old age, however, these days return with far less cynical self-mockery, with even a yearning tenderness. Alice, the shiny soft girl who sat across the aisle in study hall, returns in dreams like Botticelli's Spring, and drop-dead Billy whose hair and eyes and smile made you shiver. They enter fantasies unbidden—and then more and more bidden—as years pass.

Why do they return? What do they call you toward by coming back at this too-late hour? In fact, what is "return," which plays such a part in last years? Return to the old country, to the streets of childhood, the lovers of yesteryear, old teachers, first babies.

These feelings express the myth of Eternal Return. The great writers on myth say there is a nonplace or utopia—Paradise or Heaven or Eden or the Elysian Fields—or, more vaguely, a beyond across the river of reality, which can be reached through the death of reality and by ending the flow of time. The soul longs to break out of the clock time that governs the aging of the body so as to find again a moment of utopia. Myths imagine that as time shortens and reality fades in older age, the soul is beginning its return to this other side of which it has inklings. The return is alluring; glimpses of another place and another time become more frequent, more vivid.

To disparage the desire to return as a death wish, to psychoanalyze it as regressive idealization and retreat from reality, as sentimental nostalgia, as a useless longing for youth, cheapens the emotion—which is, in any case, enough of an embarrassment for a person eighty years old! We are captivated, irresistibly. The whole old heart sings for it; sometimes this yearning first breaks in as a phrase or lyric from an old song, as if a message from the other side.

The main messengers usually emerge from high school, like

Alice and Billy, reminding us of something changeless. They are the return of the eternal, for Alice and Billy still shine as ideal images, even if Alice grew tough and coarse and Billy OD'd in a crack house.

The myth of Eternal Return is based on a radical premise: time is cyclical. What happens now has happened before and will happen again at some basic level if not exactly in each detail. This cyclical repetition reflects the eternal time of the cosmos. Stable, sacred patterns or archetypal forces govern the changing life of the world. Life in the world moves forward in secular time, usually quite ignorant of the mythic patterns it is repeating and cannot escape from. We do not see that the new is the old come around again, and that to understand the new we must return to the old.

Scholars of the myth contrast two kinds of time, secular and sacred, rational and mystical, forward-moving time and timeless circularity. I like the way my favorite philosopher, Plotinus, makes the contrast, because his metaphysical speculations are more psychological. Plotinus says that "the forward path is characteristic of the body"; "the body tend[s] toward the straight line."[1] The soul, however, moves in circles. It circles "towards itself, the movement of self-concentrated awareness, of intellection, of the living of its life, reaching to all things so that nothing shall lie outside of it, nothing anywhere but [is] within its scope." Because of these different kinds of movements, the soul "restrains" the body's forwardness, says Plotinus. This restraining power of the soul shows up in those subtle intervening moments of hesitation in the midst of the business of life.

There is another beautiful message coded into this geometric metaphor which contrasts circles and straight lines. If you want your life not to stray too far from your soul, you need to make constant tiny adjustments so that your line of action does not go off at a tangent from the circle of the soul. In these constant adjustments by which we try to keep soul and body in touch, we are much like the sailor with his hand on the tiller, correcting course, now this side, now that, all day long. The sailor knows he is never quite on course, always a little off, always in need of small adjustments.

Correcting course all day long: This is the beginning of wisdom. It is a practice, a quiet noticing of where you actually are, not of being right on, but of being slightly off. The Greek word *sophia,* wisdom ("philosophy," love of wisdom), originally means skill in a craft such as that of the helmsman. The wisdom of the body keeps its alignment with soul by noticing when they diverge.

If the circling soul reaches all things in the living of its life, as Plotinus says, then everything, every moment, can provide psychological insight. As the soul circles, it returns again and again to the same central concern of character—honor, dignity, courage, grace, value. If our actions take us too far forward in a direct line, we get ahead of ourselves; we are no longer circling around the issues central to the soul. Then a desire arises to return to those central concerns. Hence high school, where beauty first struck, where justice became a passionate issue, where honor was in danger of compromise, where courage was demanded . . . and both madness and transcendence envisioned.

Eternal Return also means turning toward the eternal. Many myths from many cultures say that the soul's first home is an imaginal utopia (nonplace), toward which we always yearn even if we have been rooting ourselves in this earth for ninety-odd years. Greek philosophy's word for this turning toward the source is *epistrophé* (converting, twisting, sudden turning). Part of a philosopher's task was to convert haphazard events into significance by offering a fundamental idea that lifts barren facts from their literalness.

Like these so-called esoteric philosophers, I am practicing *epistrophé* throughout this book. Psychologists do this all the time. We ground senseless symptoms in deeper reasons by leading those symptoms back to meaningful sources in the psyche. This book twists conventional ideas about aging, attempting to convert much of what plagues later years into intelligible insight. We are trying to find a home for our happenings. The facts of aging become more understandable when brought back to soul, which can give them value. A symptom suffers most when it doesn't know where it belongs.

The desire for an undefinable elsewhere keeps one slightly estranged, unplanted, subject to inexplicable feelings of exile to which psychology gives names like "loneliness" and "abandonment." The old are told to get more involved. Yet engagement with other earthlings does not assuage *unearthly* longings. These are not longings for this world and they are not satisfied by anything we do anywhere with anybody. In fact, these yearnings often come all of a sudden, in the midst of friends and family, in the arms of a lover.

These feelings represent the utopian impulse, the soul's urge to return, its homesickness for a realm that cannot be encompassed by logic or pragmatism. So the return to primordial beauty continues to call the heart despite our skeptical judgment and vulnerable embarrassment. Since our modern systems of understanding leave a void regarding the realities of the soul, we have no images for what this *epistrophé* wants. We do not know where to locate this place or how to receive its communications. All we have of this place left behind is high school and its angelic seductions; Billy and Alice. The primordial enclosure before time began becomes imprisonment in pristine adolescence.

The spontaneous return of a utopian place and time to our nodding daydreams may be preparation for leaving for soul country. Whether there *is* such a place, whether there is even a soul, or a home that is its source and destination, no one will ever prove or know. The one returning witness who could have told us facts and stimulated research was Lazarus, who had been dead for four days and was already decomposed when Jesus brought him back. But Lazarus was never debriefed.

We do have myths. Myths nourish the old soul with even older stories. They give us strange images and amazing suggestions; these promote speculations that activate the aging mind. To go beyond speculations is to become a preacher of theology who can tell you about life after death, or a metaphysician who can postulate energy transformations, reincarnations, karmic justice, intrauterine existence, past life, channeled information. All revelations are dangerous when taken literally, but remain valid and beautiful as anecdotes of the marvelous. The psychologist more timidly retreats, though not as a cynical skeptic, simply wishing to remain here on earth among the questions rather than go beyond for answers. For evidence of the elsewhere we do not need to go elsewhere. Evidence is not the point; desire is. Maybe the desire *is* the evidence.

Billy and Alice: From the ancient viewpoint and the mystical one as well, their images would be nothing less than summoning angels. Of course, their apparitions make you melt and shiver; their allure is ever fetching; of course, they do not age with the passing of time. Of course, too, psychological explanations fall flat at their feet, powerless against them.

Does this returning power of an ordinary human from an ordinary worldly place, high school, still kept as an image in the heart's locket, say something about your own destiny? Could you, too, become a revenant in someone else's heart? Alice and Billy may be intimations of immortality: your own. Are you becoming like them, timeless, your image never fading, shed of bothersome infirmity, with very little reality, a nowhere person, utopian? Reduced to a mere wisp, your essence becomes finally only a character in others' dramas, as Billy and Alice are in yours.

In his late years, the French writer André Gide questioned whether there was any reality left him at all: "Yesterday in the train I suddenly found myself quite sincerely wondering whether I was really still alive." At another moment, he wrote: "It is a long time now since I ceased to exist. I merely fill the place of someone they take for me."[2] All the while, as he is leaving worldly reality and perceiving this withdrawal (which psychiatry calls depersonalization), he is more and more filling a place as an imaginary figure in the history of literature, one of those writers once referred to as the Immortals. Gide the man is undergoing a kind of *epistrophé.* His human being is reverting to his calling. Is this why old people seem to shrink and evaporate? "When I saw her last," we say, "she was just a ghost of her-self." As Gide the man leaves the scene, what fills his place and continues to live on is Gide the image; *that* settles down per-manently in the home of imagination, much like a character in one of his novels. Character displaces person.

INTERLUDE

THE FORCE
OF THE FACE

. . . honour the face of the old man . . .

Leviticus 19:32

The Force of the Face

For by his face straight shall you know his heart.
Shakespeare, Richard III

Baby Face/Death Mask. Right away, at birth, the infant no sooner delivered, breathing, and bathed, its face is studied for clues to character. It looks so fierce, so wisely old, so placid, so much like "your" side of the family. . . . And, at the end, quiescent and struggle-free on the deathbed, they used to come with the plaster to make a death mask. The custom, begun almost five thousand years ago in Egypt, would capture the essence of character in the features of the face.

Psychology Loses Face. Eleven authoritative texts on identity, self, personality, ego, and subject: no mention of the face; "character" unfound in the indexes.

Ishmael Looks at Queequeg. Does the face reveal character or hide it? At the Spouter-Inn Ishmael beds down with Queequeg before they sail off to hunt for Moby Dick, the white whale. At first sight of his roommate, a cannibal harpooner, Ishmael is frightened:

Good heavens! what a sight! Such a face! It was of a dark, purplish, yellow color, here and there stuck over with large, black-
ish looking squares. . . . There was no hair on his head—none
to speak of at least—nothing but a small scalp-knot twisted up
on his forehead. His bald purplish head now looked for all the
world like a mildewed skull.[1]

Then, later, as Ishmael's fears abate, he looks again at "the
savage":

With much interest I sat watching him. Savage though he was,
and hideously marred about the face—at least to my taste—his
countenance yet had a something in it which was by no means
disagreeable. You cannot hide the soul. Through all his unearthly tattooings, I thought I saw the traces of a simple honest heart; and in his large, deep eyes, fiery black and bold, there
seemed tokens of a spirit that would dare a thousand devils.
And besides all this, there was a certain lofty bearing about the
Pagan, which even his uncouthness could not altogether
maim. . . . [H]is head was phrenologically an excellent one.[2]

Tattoos, odd hairdress, and the colored skin make Ishmael
want to bolt for the door. But he returns to the face "with much
interest." He looks again, an act that literally initiates a new
"re-gard," a fresh "re-spect." He begins to see through the
"hideously marred face," or see what comes through it. But
this can happen only after he sits and watches; only after he
calls upon his idea of soul does he imagine traces of form
and value within the visible head. Ishmael already had an *idea*
of character, and so he could see soul, heart, depth, spirit, or
bearing—the words Melville attributes to Ishmael's perception
of Queequeg. To see character we must look for it with an idea
of character.

Facial Courage. "I want to grow old without facelifts. They
take the life out of a face, the character. I want to have the
courage to be loyal to the face I've made," said Marilyn Monroe.[3] That's one kind of courage. Another kind is exhibited by

Joyce Nash, Ph.D., who describes her facelift in detail. "Most patients underestimate the amount of pain and physical trauma involved in cosmetic surgery. They are also unprepared for the depression that may ensue."[4]

Trauma? Besides the acute postoperative distress, which passed in time, there were long-term effects. Nash had trouble wearing earrings, because her earlobes were sutured to the surrounding skin. Her glasses no longer held behind her ears. Her jaw was permanently discolored, and she had the sensation that a strap was cinched tight under her chin and over her skull.

Depression? "What I saw was disturbing. It didn't look like me, and it didn't feel like me. Something was lost. A sense of sadness welled up. . . . The frown lines, the sleepy look, the sagging cheeks and neck were gone."

The American Academy of Cosmetic Surgeons reports that 72 percent of those who consult cosmetic surgeons are interested in facial work. In 1996 more than half a million people had some kind of facial cosmetic surgery. Here we might distinguish between cosmetic plastic surgery that is mainly intended to rectify the signs of aging, and reconstructive plastic surgery that aims at improved socialization, following a disfiguring accident or birth defect.

Nash had surgery for cosmetic reasons. She sums up the result: "The face I see in the mirror now belies my actual age, and it better reflects how I feel inside. I have accepted . . . all permanent reminders of my surgery in return for the improved appearance."[5] For Nash an "improved appearance" means that her outside accords with her inside and she no longer looks her age. Was the former discrepancy the fault of the outside, or of an inside that had not kept pace with her face? She had the courage to go through the operation, but not the courage to let aging form her face by what the philosopher Emmanuel Levinas called "passive synthesis."[6] She could not yield to the "thematic harmony" (Roland Barthes's phrase) that aging is achieving. For her, the artificial distortions brought on by surgery were improvements over the frown lines, the sleepy look.[7]

Barthes makes a useful distinction between the *chronos* of

biology and the *chronos* of passion, such as we see in Rembrandt's late self-portraits where the ravages depicted are due less to the passing of time than to the effects of passion. It is these effects in the face, the transmission to it of the passions of character, that Monroe hoped to have the courage to face. She spoke not of the biological face she was given, but the face "I've made." Anna Magnani, the great postwar Italian actress of passions, supposedly told the makeup man doing her face for a scene: "Don't take out a single line. I paid for each one."

Nash's "improved appearance" treats the face as a new and improved product, according not only with the younger age she feels, but with standardized notions of appearance. Her postoperative image adapts to conventional imagery; is that also the image of her character? Has she abandoned her uniqueness, sold her soul?

The depression that ensued gives a clue as to how the soul regards the alteration of the face, the loss of its peculiar, if sagging, individuality. Nash refers the sadness to the loss of her old face. The depression, however, also brings tidings of what she was gaining: the sense of the soul's reality that always comes with sadness, and that notices what we do with our faces.

"Smile, that's the thing to do. . . ." To build character, "do something for no other reason than its difficulty," said William James.[8] Difficulty uses the face; it furrows the brow, tenses the eyes, purses the lips. Focus, concentration, effort. In James's times family photos and group portraits were gravely serious. "Wipe that smile off your face" was meant not only for soldiers. Then along came Kodak, and smiling became de rigueur. The face prefers to smile. Frowning and scowling take more muscle. The culture's actual face has been easing slowly into a copy of its smiling photograph. If deficit attention and learning disability are increasing, let's look to the little yellow "happy face" as contributing cause. The attention needed for learning hardly starts off with the imperative "Have a nice day!"

Expression, an Aesthetic Phenomenon. Not because of cosmetics and surgery is the face an aesthetic phenomenon, but because it is biologically so. Besides the muscles needed functionally to chew, kiss, sniff, blow, squint, blink, and twitch away a fly, most of the forty-five facial muscles serve only emotional expression. You don't need them to bring in food, to beat down an enemy, nurse an offspring, or perform sexual intercourse. The ventriloquist proves they are not needed for speaking. Nor are they essential to breathing, hearing, or sleeping. The extravagance of facial musculature is all for expression of major emotions, yes; but even more for such peculiar subtleties of civilization as supercilious contempt, wry irony, wide-eyed fawning, cool unconcern, smiling, and sneering.

By means of these muscles, our faces make pictures. The psyche displays aesthetically its states of soul. Character traits become intelligible images; yet each expression is characteristically different, and the more complex the character, the more individual the expression. "There is nothing average about expression. It is essentially individual. In so far as an average dominates, expression fades."[9]

If we conceive facial expressions only as Darwin did, they are evolutionary remnants of preverbal communication. "Basic" emotions, such as fear, surprise, and anger are the least individualized, the most average—and *the least expressive,* if we follow Whitehead. The multitudinous face is required for aesthetic precision. This idea appears in an aesthetic principle set forth by the English philosopher T. E. Hulme: "You could define art as a passionate desire for accuracy."[10] Fear, surprise, and anger express only "that part of the emotion which is common to all of us. If you are able to observe the actual individuality of the emotion you become dissatisfied with language"—and unsatisfied by Darwinian reduction. Although it may capture the animal background of expression, it fails the psyche's individualized expressiveness. Besides, we are left wondering about the source of those expressions, which animals do not have the facial muscles to display: laughing and weeping; orgasmic, mystical, and sadistic ecstasy; paranoid suspicion.

Character Seeps Through the Cracks. Will his jaw quiver, a tear emerge? Will his eyes shift away or narrow slightly? We watch the face for tell-tale signs. Portraits decorating the halls of corporate power and in the annual reports show faces with no cracks. Nothing seeps through. Is there nothing to seep through, or does this unrevealing face reveal the essential character of corporate power?

The Face Animates. Halloween is indeed a Pagan festival, as severe Christians declare, banning its costumed fun from many schools. It's Pagan not because of witches but because of pumpkins, whose faces flicker with an inner light. Animism: character in the nonhuman, soul in vegetables.

Disfigurement. An accident, a burn, a war wound, or partial paralysis from a stroke and the face suffers radical alteration. Is character altered because the face has changed?

Two fictions—*The Man in the Iron Mask* and *The Elephant Man*—suggest that the resources of character lie concealed from view. What you see is not altogether what you get. As their faces are locked, stiffened, or grossly distorted, their characters seem nonetheless to deepen and become more resolute. Face and character must not coincide; then how conceive their relation? Not as one of identity; as interplay. Aging intensifies the partnership. In old age, they marry.

The Invisible Face. Phrenology's mistake lay in trying to capture and measure invisible character in the visible face. Form as shaping principle and form as visible shape are co-relative, but not identical. The essential reality of one's image is more like an angel or a daimon, not empirical, not measurable, not visible, only imaginable. Even J. K. Lavater of Zurich, the eighteenth-century founder of phrenology, insisted that it took a gifted imagination to apply his rules for reading character. Each face is different—not only because of its individuality, but because of its essential invisibility.

Facing Old Age. As we get very old, our mind wanders among images and we are brought back to our bodies by infirmities and the caring attention or neglect of others. As our bodies shrivel, we become our faces. Feet, hams, arms, and shoulders lose their shapeliness, while the face gains distinction, even beauty. The old naked body is unsightly, yet its naked face is a subject for long contemplation. The sagging skin and webbing veins on the body tell only of old age, while on the face they enter the composite portrait and contribute to its significance, sometimes its magnificence. The face makes visible the metamorphosis of biology into art.

Definition. "A face, in the end, is the place where the coherent mind becomes an image."[11] What enters into that coherence? A coalition of flickering displays: the ancestral forces of genetics, the history of personal passions, the ravages of fate, geographies and climates, daimonic intentions and societal compliances.

The Bare Face. "Prior to any particular expression and beneath all particular expressions . . . there is the nakedness and destitution of the expression as such, that is to say the extreme exposure, defencelessness, vulnerability itself . . . a mysterious forsakenness."[12] "The face of man is the medium through which the invisible in him becomes visible and enters into commerce with us."[13]

According to Emmanuel Levinas, the most radical, soulful, and profoundly positive French thinker of the last fifty years, the human face as an archetypal phenomenon bears one message: utter vulnerability. Therefore, the face will be disguised, covered, decorated, surgically altered—or, on the contrary, deprived of all possibilities of hiding, as in the abject condition of prisoner, captive, and victim.

This is also why our faces are so impossibly difficult to accept: We are staring into "vulnerability itself." In the face is our forsakenness, our exile. Age has nothing to do with it. Teenagers flock to plastic surgeons to have their faces changed—those young faces the old wish they had again! They flock to return from exile, to be one with the crowd, to end the condition of extreme exposure; they want to remedy the face that has begun to exteriorize their unique individuality.

Although the teenager doesn't yet know it, that vulnerability, that nakedness is the face's greatest appeal, its true beauty. Witness Marilyn Monroe, whose attraction lay not in the proportions of her features but in the mysterious forsakenness her face revealed. Even if gladdened and tautened and lifted out of its destitution, a face remains the visage of mystery. It is soul present as an image, soul in all its vulnerability. For Levinas, the face expresses a sacred power.

Just here, with the face, ethics begins, and Levinas's philosophy of radical altruism. The source of ethical existence is the face of the other, its appeal for response. To it we are instinctively, archetypally responsive and responsible. It claims recognition; it must be addressed, encountered. A face offers itself, gives itself, and calls me out of myself. "The Other becomes my neighbour precisely through the way the face summons me," says Levinas.[14] Contrary to Descartes, who starts with his own private interior ego ("I think, therefore I am"), Levinas starts with the Other's face. "The face opens the primordial discourse whose first word is obligation,"[15] from which follows the ethics of justice, compassion, shame, and honesty. "When the Other faces me, then I am more likely to be honest than when privately reflecting."[16]

The Other's face calls upon my character. Rather than thinking that my character shows in my face and that my face is my character exteriorized, Levinas asks us to think that character requires the face of the Other. Its piercing provocation pulls from us every possible ethical potential. In bad conscience we turn away from the face in the wheelchair, the face of the beggar; we hood the face of the executed, and we ignore the faces of the socially ostracized and hierarchically inferior so that they become "invisible" even as we walk down the same street. Levinas's thought also suggests that ethics cannot be injected into character by moral precepts, or taught or trained, or even modeled by superior masters. Character is already inherently ethical, awaiting only to be exteriorized by the encounter with the vulnerable face of the Other. Example: Queequeg's face evokes Ishmael's virtues.

God's Face. The presence of the Biblical god is in his countenance. Jewish prayers often repeat phrases from the Psalms and Numbers: "The Lord make his face to shine upon thee. . . . The Lord incline his countenance unto thee," says the New Year's service.[17] But in Jewish tradition it is often said God's face cannot be seen (except by Moses); or, as Christians later said, God's face is mirrored in nature. If this be the case, then no set of virtues and powers could present his character of multitudinous profligacy as well as could a face such as those by the Milan painter Arcimboldo (1527–93), composed of flowers, leaves, and vegetables of every sort.

Jewish mystics say that God hides his face because the direct force of its glory would burn creation. He must remain hidden (*deus absconditus*), unknowable, and withdrawn (*tsim tsum*) to allow space for creation. Therefore by his side on the throne is Metatron, the first of the angels, "the prince of the divine face" (*sar ha-panim*).[18] If we humans are made in the likeness of God, as the Bible says, then we must be as essentially invisible as he is. The nearest we can get to discovering our God-like image must be the face, since the Face Angel is the closest to God's throne. That angel gives the face its force, "a force," says Levinas, "that convinces the people who do not wish to listen."[19] Angels announce, report, and bear messages. That is what the Greek root *aggelos* means. My face announces my presence, reports my nature, and above all, by facing outward, bears a message for others. Angels blow trumpets. They call for awakening. So does the face; it demands response. Myths and *midrashim* of this sort lie at the back of Levinas's ethical metaphysics.

Hamlet to Gertrude. "You go not, till I set up a glass / Where you may see the inmost part of you."

The face reveals character. The mirror does not lie.

Yet Eliot, another observant poet, claims the face to be precisely where we can and do dissemble: "Time to prepare a face to meet the faces that you meet."[20] The face both reveals and conceals. Is it possible to control the revelations for a desired effect, and if so, are these truly revelations, or, more likely, manipulations? Marilyn Monroe said: "I can make my face do anything I want."

In highly ceremonial traditions, whether "tribal" or civilized"—the royally formalist Arab societies, eighteenth-century France, the Mandarin court—the face never shows one's inmost part. It must be tacit. Control of the face means self-possession; it means subjugation of the inmost parts, conceived as vicious and bestial or at least uncivilized. Reserve represents mastery.[21] The accoutrements of fashion are not merely fashion, decorations for attraction or even expression. Wigs, powders, veils and headdresses, well-groomed facial hair, beauty marks aid in keeping the face under control, lest inmost parts be seen. Especially servants will be uniformed—the men shaven, the women under bonnets. The art of the face as the art of disguise, a triumph of the persona, significations that hide the signifier.

Romanticism freed the inmost part and broke with this facial style, as did the hippies of the sixties; with their long and unruly hair, their cheeks and lips unshaven and unrouged, they faced off against the classically composed world of IBM suits, Debbie Reynolds perms, and the military jaw.

Classical versus Romantic; controlled versus expressive. But what about the inmost part?

The transparencies of emotion passing through the face of the Norwegian actress Liv Ullmann, filmed so revealingly by Ingmar Bergman, were all for the camera. They were *acted* expressions. Had she made visible her inmost part? Or was she "merely" acting a character? And—unless her character called her to be an actress—then, like Marilyn Monroe, was she not using her face rather than revealing it? Besides, was there an inmost part not available to her face, like the prostitute who maintains her virginity by always holding inviolate some place, word, act, or feeling symbolic of the inmost part?

Hamlet Corrected by Proust. "The human face is really like one of those Oriental gods: a whole group of faces juxtaposed on different planes; it is impossible to see them all simultaneously," said Proust. We must watch a face over time, in shifting lights, through many scenes. No one has "a" face. Gertrude's inmost part cannot be caught in a single mirror only. The old face displays the superimposition of the "whole group of faces." All seven ages passing and repassing, a texture to be read between the lines. Even a baby's face intimates this range; fleeting expressions of dispositions unrealized, but possible.

Swift Agrees with Hamlet. A sermon attributed to Jonathan Swift, "On the Difficulty of Knowing One's Self," says you must have a reflective mirror to achieve self-knowledge: "A Man can no more know his own Heart than he can know his own Face, any other Way than by Reflection." For Swift this reflection comes from the regard of others.

Wilde Disagrees with Both Swift and Hamlet. "Man is least himself when he talks in his own person. Give him a mask [not a mirror] and he will tell the truth."

Goethe Concurs with Wilde. " 'Know Thyself'? If I knew myself, I'd run away."

Break the Mirror

> In the morning
> After taking cold shower
> —What a mistake—
> I look at the mirror.
>
> There, a funny guy,
> Grey hair, white beard, wrinkled skin,
> —What a pity—
> Poor, dirty, old man!
> He is not me, absolutely not.
>
> Land and life
> Fishing in the ocean
> Sleeping in the desert with stars
> Building a shelter in mountains
> Farming the ancient way

Singing with coyotes
Singing against nuclear war—
I'll never be tired of life.
Now I'm seventeen years old,
Very charming young man.

I sit down quietly in lotus position,
Meditating, meditating for nothing.
Suddenly a voice comes to me:

"To stay young,
To save the world,
Break the mirror."[22]

Mirror, Mirror on the Wall. Mostly what the mirror shows is not the inmost part but the outer face of aging. A glanced reflection in a shop window, the face seen in a mirror at an odd angle supposedly brings "the first disturbing awareness of aging."[23] Freud had this disturbing recognition: While he was traveling on a train, an elderly person suddenly entered his compartment. But it was Freud himself. He had caught sight of his head in the compartment mirror behind the door, flung open by the train's sudden movement. He was repulsed by his own reflection. Similarly Wagner: He angrily rejected what caught his eye in a shop window. "I do not recognize myself in that gray-head!"[24]

Why the shock? Is it purely a refusal to witness the fact of age, or a refusal of something else? The face itself? Do I suddenly see my mother? But it's me, O Lord! Not my mother, not my sister, really me, O Lord! "After a certain age," said Proust, "the more one becomes oneself, the more obvious one's family traits become." Owning our own faces = becoming more individualized = owning our ancestry. At any age the sudden mirror holds the same surprise. "I did not know I looked like that!" I tear up the snapshot, destroy the video of an off-moment conversation. I want the recorded image to conform with and reaffirm the invisible image I feel to be "me." So it is not the marks of age as such that I cannot bear, but the documented revelation of my cherished illusion: that my face presents my character. I want the invisible image of "me" to be truly present in the mirror. The mirror leaves out too much. Mirrors cannot tell the whole truth, and therefore they always lie.

The Whole Truth. What do the mirrors leave out? Why can that reflected image never be just right? Yeats explains:

> From mirror after mirror
> No vanity's displayed
> I'm looking for the face I had
> Before the world was made.[25]

The primordial image embracing your whole character remains incomplete because you are still living and it is still taking shape. The whole character cannot ever show. The only true image is that which appears momentarily. So we look and look again in "mirror after mirror."

Characters Without Faces. Many writers purposely omit descriptions of their characters' faces. The reader pieces together their character from their names, actions, and conversations, and from others' views of them. The novel can proceed without the author bothering with the hero's fine complexion or the villain's hooded eyes and stumpy teeth. The figures who people stories become characters through imagination. We imagine them into visibility, but their essence is a complex invisible image. When the novel turns into a movie, the visible face never quite fits the imagined character. No matter how exquisitely Audrey Hepburn plays Natasha in *War and Peace,* we leave the theater having seen Audrey Hepburn, not Natasha. The literary fiction does not altogether yield to literal filming. In none of us who act our entries and exits on the world's stage can character be made altogether visible without compromising the invisibility that is essential to the fascination of character and forces us to imagine it.

"Faces need to be used." "A face is something that is incomplete: a work in progress . . . faces need to be used because they are not finished images," says the Chicago art historian James Elkins.[26] Aging as a progress of the face. If you consider your face as one more part of the body, then it withers, crinkles, blotches, and falls away like other parts of the body. If you imagine your face as a phenomenon with a different significance, with its own destiny, then all that goes on there, after sixty especially, is a work in progress, building the image, preparing a face that has little to do with the faces that you meet. What's going on, rather, is the progress of a portrait, toward a memory.

"Faces need to be used." How? Out there, weathering and leathering, actively engaged with world? Should we engage in full-face confrontations, get in each other's faces? Another way to use the face is aging. Aging uses the face every day, and it is these traces of use that cosmetic surgery sets out to repair. Without any effort on our part, quite passively, even in the solitude of a monk's cell, even in an immune-protective bubble, the face is being used. "The aging process," says Levinas, "is probably the most perfect model of passive synthesis."[27] A face is being made, often against your will, as witness to your character.

Jung and Freud. Jung did more than relativize Freud's theories of childhood, sexuality, and development. He relativized the power of the analyst by opening analysis to the face. He moved the analyst's chair from behind the reclining patient to a position across from the seated patient. Patient and analyst, two armchairs, face-to-face. Concealment and disclosure shifted to the present reciprocal gaze. The unconscious was now present in the terrifying difficulty of the encounter.

If your face is not a finished image, then psychoanalysis may provide occasions to finish it, to work on your face. The patient seeks to release or compose a face that does not impede the changes in character that analysis fosters. However, the Freudian face seems a finished image like the bust of Freud on the mantel of the consulting room, like the photo of Freud on the wall with the diplomas, like the male analyst's beard. When analysts sit behind the patient, employing Freud's face-less method, they take on the image of Freud, *imitatio dei,* and practice a method analogous to the International Style of architecture, universally functional anywhere and serviceable to any client.

Jung's Face. A group of students at the Jung Institute in Zurich went to Jung's house for conversation with the ancestor of our discipline. He was then in his eighties. Someone asked him an abstract question about the shadow. He went right at it. Putting his hand to his cheek, he said, "It is right here." The shadow was not a concept, not a theory, not lurking behind a curtain: a living force in the face.

The Face of the World. "The world lives in order to develop the lines on its face," says T. E. Hulme.[28] Repeat: *its* face. Not only humans have faces. We do not own them all. The man in the moon, faces in clouds, profiles in rocks, eyes staring out of tree trunks, carrots, potatoes . . . Buildings show off their facades and surface skins; they face each other across the downtown streets. Ancient Egyptians imagined the sky as a vast face with the sun and moon as eyes. The Navaho say something is always watching us.

If we no longer imagine that "objects stare back," then the things around us spark no ethical challenge, make no appeal. They are not partners in dialogue with whom an I-Thou relationship obtains. Once the soul of the world loses its face, we see things rather than images. Things ask no more of us than to be owned and used, becoming possessions.

The lost face of the world is not mentioned by environmentalists. Like their opponents, the harvesters, exploiters, and developers, they read the world according to their desires. Sustainability, conservation, and restoration are noble programs, but still the human is in charge and the world is merely the arena where we implement our plans. Instead, environmentalism needs to read the lines in the face of the world, read each piece of the world for its character, to study its development and be struck to the heart by its defenselessness.

To be attentive and only attentive would slow action. Hence environmental studies are slow to report conclusions. There is no quick read of the lines on the world's face. Each bit needs the assiduous attention of the portraitist, the landscapist. They read the lines and read between the lines. Is that why Constable, Cezanne, and Monet are truly so important? Each gave years to the face of one small bit of the world, a mini-bioregion. Art historians consider them founders of Impressionism, of Cubism; I see their work as the beginning of environmental painting. Each was a character painter in search of the invisible image in the visible lines of the world's face.

Losing Face in America. If the face is where the ethics of society begins, then what happens to a society when the aging face is surgically altered, cosmetically subdued, and its accumulated character falsified? What ethical damage occurs when the faces of elders are rarely on view? Or if the old faces on view are those that have been plucked, tucked, and brought on camera to authenticate a product? Or those that have not been improved and appear wretched enough to sentimentalize.

For the good of society, should cosmetic facelifts be prohibited? Are they a crime against humanity? What you do to your visible image has societal implications. Your face is the Other for everyone else. If it no longer bares its essential vulnerability, then the grounds for caring, the demand for honesty, the call to respond on which societal cohesion rests have lost their originating source.

This ground for the crisis in American integrity is never discussed. Yet the cover-up of the aging American face may be more the reason for ethical decay than the liberating movements of the 1960s, which supposedly corrupted family values and bent the moral backbone of America into its present "perverted" condition. Rather than standing on high moral ground and exposing the faults around them, the older generation would do better to expose the fault lines in their own faces.

What the old can do for society lies in their hands: They can help, they can give, they can instruct. It also lies in their feet: They can march, they can vote, they can go out to local meetings. Mostly it lies in their faces, in the courage to be seen.

We have few ready images of the compelling intensity of soul. There are so few faces to point to, no visible ancestors to anchor the community. Who on TV can we look at and be struck to the soul? If we're to see character, someone has to impersonate Lincoln! What public figure can put a nation back on track just by force of character as shown in an older face? Without such elders, we are left with reprimanding bullies and pulpit hysterics whose faces belie the virtues they profess. Chiefs, shamans, elders, rabbis, dons, doges, bonzes, bishops, the antique masters of disciplined studies commanded the respect of their communities by the presence of character shown in their faces. Not all, not always—but at least they embodied the idea that the face of the old belongs to the group. To gain his troops' allegiance, a new Caesar in Rome had to walk among them, reveal himself to them. Words and deeds and photo opportunities cannot encompass the full measure of character; we need to see at length and often. We look at each other to see into each other. Of course we misjudge and follow the wrong perceptions, but these errors do not negate the idea that it is a citizen's duty to make his face public. Only God may hide his face.

III

LEFT

"Night is now falling fast," said Goff;
"Soon it will be quite dark."
"Then we shall all go home," said Mr. Hackett.

Samuel Beckett, Watt

CHAPTER 17

From "Leaving" to "Left"

Suppose you exchange the word "leaving" for "dying" and substitute "preparing" for "aging." Then what we go through in our last years is preparation for departure. This is the simplest way of conceiving the transition from "leaving" to "left." We slow down and go over things in our minds because there is so much to prepare. As the soul comes into the world slowly, taking all the years of childhood to adjust, so it leaves the world slowly, requiring years of old age to pack up and take off.

I find this way of thinking far from helpful. Its simplicity cheats human life of complexity in late years, and, being simple, it is also dangerous. The dangers are three: First, by turning all thoughts about leaving to death, it takes our thoughts away from life. Second, it diverts our curiosity from the adventure of this life toward metaphysical questions about the next—afterlife, reincarnation, heaven and hell, and other supposed signals from the far side of the river. Third, it raises no questions about what is left after *you* have left.

Let us stay on this side and look more closely into "left." "Left" is the past participle of "leave," which we can say in two different ways: "*has* left" and "*is* left." The first means "not here, gone"; the second, "still here, remains." Can we be gone and still remain?

We could say that the body remains and the soul departs; or that the body disintegrates while the soul remains imperishable. Because we cannot easily hold the two together, they divide along an ancient fault line underlying our culture: the separation of body and soul. Does the body remain in an urn of ashes while the soul floats off to an eternal kingdom? Or is nothing left once you have left? There are invariably disputes about what *is* left—disposal of the body, the estate. And about what *has* left. Where have you gone to; where are you now? Is there another life? Can you come back; will you?

Could we join these two senses of "left"? Can we imagine both going and staying?

I propose that we give up the simplistic opposition between body and soul, and instead imagine a unique character encapsulated in images. These images have bodily shape and act like bodily forces. They can sound in your ears and walk through your dreams, and their enduring strength can affect your habits, tastes, and decisions for years after the person who was the first source of these images has left the stage. A character comes to life with elements of body and soul and is reducible to neither, not even to both. Character is an independent configuration, neither the body in the grave nor the soul bound for its theological destination.

Your mother, for instance—or a deceased husband, a lover, a teacher, a very dear friend, a person you knew only slightly—has left, and yet remains as a force of character. People's images survive their passing and, sometimes, have more power after they have left.

These images are not merely memories, purely, subjectively *yours;* they show surprising autonomy. They come uninvited right in the middle of a choice, whispering advice, disapproval, criticism. They inspire. They tempt with longing. They hold us to opinions that we might have abandoned long ago. They compel us to hang on to inconsequential objects that crowd our closets and drawers because these things act on us like remains of that character and are imbued with its staying power. "I can't

just throw this out!" And, if we finally do, the act is heavy, cere-
monious, like a ritual.

You may little suspect the fullness of someone's character
just from reviewing your memories. Your father's character,
say, goes on unfolding and you go on learning about him, from
him. He returns to mind in flashbacks and reveries. As you age,
and you become more like him, he often feels nearer. A glimpse
in the mirror, a dish in a restaurant, a joke in an old movie, and
traits of his light up, never having been noticed before. Under
scrutiny, the images reveal more and more, revising the obituary, nuancing impressions, teaching still.

Long before you have left, you already comprise a tangle of
images that compress your complexity into a "character," affecting others as an imaginative vital force. Because we do
not imagine the image others perceive, we hardly know the impact of our own character. Images of this character enter the
dreams and thoughts of others, sparking a response, awakening
a feeling, raising a question, as if trying to call them to something.

So, what is left of you after you have left is character, the
layered image that has been shaping your potentials and your
limits from the beginning. Later years define this character
more clearly as the repetitive stories and erotic fantasies, the
nighttime vigils and the haunting searches through the halls of
memory force the singularity of our character upon us. Left in
a chair, parked on a bench, our reach restricted, our energy uncertain, we are more and more reduced to the images that we
have become, "Those images that yet / Fresh images beget."[1]

———

To be left. This possibility haunts any intimate union, especially
the close friendships that marriages often become. Fantasies of
being the one left out, left over, left behind, left alone creep into
a marriage right from its beginning, suggested by the words in
the vows: "sickness," "forsaking," "death," "part." With union
comes the possibility of disunion, deception, desertion, divorce. Even before any distancing begins, the archetypal condition of being left can put us on the rack. The anxieties are not

reducible to those occasioned by childhood fears of abandonment. Being left is wholly an adult condition, inherent in marriage and growing with its anniversaries.

The myths and cults of the Greek goddess of marriage, Hera, speak directly to this misery. Hera had three principal forms, corresponding with three phases of the moon—waxing, full, and waning; and three landscapes of her cult (at Stymphalos)—mountain, city, and lowland swamp. The three faces of Hera's presence—girl-bride, fulfilled woman, and widow—correspond to the terrain of her cult.[2]

The waning phase, metaphorically appropriate to lowland swamp and dimming lunar light, bears directly on being left. "Chera"—one of Hera's names[3]—and its cognates have all these meanings: "widow" and "widower"; "bereft," "bereaved"; "to leave, forsake"; "to live in solitude"; "exile"; and, also, "need" and "in want." Today we might add "homeless" and "bag lady." These fantasies projected forward into old age may, however, invade at any age.

Marriage offers the homeless no true shelter. It is a porous fortress, because *chera* belongs in its foundations as Hera is its founder. So we try to wall marriage in, to build a solid home, overstuffed with joint accumulations. Do our physical dwellings and their furnishings represent ways we try to keep *chera* on the other side of the wall, out in the street, only a vague threat of being left, but not an actuality? Hera herself liked houses. The *domos* (house) and domesticity were her province. As building a house brings hope of security, so moving house evokes shattering fears of breaking up the bonding, the bondage, of domestic routines. If we can only stay put, we can stay together and never be left.

Yet wherever Hera is present, so is *chera*. Besides the yielding cow-eyed girl who never dies in the soul of the marriage, and the woman of ruling position who holds it all together and must be served, there is the eternally forsaken one who is always in want. As the goddess holds all three conditions in her one figure, inseparable, so all three potentials are present in her institution. Fantasies of being left will play through the couple even when the moon is fullest. When we marry, we marry *chera,* though on that day we may see only Hebe, Hera's young, smiling shape.

———

There is another idea of the left. This left has nothing to do with the metaphysics of dying, but it has much to offer for the understanding of aging and character. This is the political left, the left that is not right, the left that in French is *gauche,* which also means awkward, the left that in Italian is *sinistra,* which also means eerie, the left that in Spanish is *izquierdo,* which also means crooked. Cognates of "left" in Old English mean disease, paralysis; in Dutch, weak and worthless; in Middle English crippled, defective, clumsy.

We should not wonder that right-wing, straight-thinking political patriots cannot abide left-wing politics, or that the political right, as it moves toward the "far right," also moves from mild suspicion of the left to vicious intolerance. (Not long ago educators strongly believed that left-handedness had to be driven from the schools, lest it negatively affect a child's developing character.)

Later years find us often leaning toward the left as we are more often left out and left behind. Weak, defective, and clumsy, my body is already picking up leftish tendencies, and my mind has begun to move down crooked paths and to engage in strange encounters with nonconformist thoughts and feelings. I find myself becoming a fellow traveler of the oppressed, the underdogs and marginals.

Supposedly, we tighten up in old age. Scrooge becomes the standard image of the miser; an old witch eats children for dinner; the old king's moribund stagnation poisons the realm. Political cartoons for the last hundred years show the old as monopolists and imperialists, Wall Street fat cats, pompous prelates, aged admirals in golf outfits. Opinion polls seem to reinforce this right turn in old age, since the older citizens who actually vote tend to vote for morally strict, tightfisted, uncharitable conservatives. So we are led to believe.

Yet the heart has its own agenda, which comes from its own manner of aging. Individuals—even those on the political right—seem to turn left. We find charity, sweetening, praise. Endowments prompted by gratitude; donations to relieve the suffering of poverty, ignorance, and pain. A dominant theme of late years is giving back, an appreciation of how far we have come, how much we have been helped. We respond to kindness and join societies to preserve historic shrines, old animals, natural sites. We speak out in letters to the editor, in defense of causes, joining the protest. "Talent develops in solitude," said Goethe, "character in life's stream." We have progressivist visions of betterment, even as we personally may be falling apart. The disabled, the veterans, the slow learners and recidivists—these are us. We rouse ourselves from torpor so as to visit museums to see paintings that make us all but weep, and we dissolve our prejudices in great music. Are the old in church mainly because of impending death or not also for prayer, quiet, and beauty? We do raise Cain, but we also smile thanks, phone an ailing friend, feed small birds.

I think the true agenda of the old is the agenda of the left: more fairness and less profit; more restoration and less development; community care, not more prescriptions; restoration of nature, not more harvesting from it; less wrangling over Medicare and more genuine nursing; more public transportation, fewer private enclaves; investment in schools to teach the young, not prisons that let them languish; more friendliness with people rather than user-friendly electronics; and peace, not guns.

—

One of the goals of alchemists was to concoct the "elixir," a panacea that would heal all ills and prolong all lives. This miraculous substance had many names, the most inclusive being *lapis philosophorum,* philosophers' stone.

When an alchemist recommends *softening* the stone, we want to listen since this description runs counter to the entrenched habits of our thinking about stones and against our belief that the surest way to last is to become a tough character, like a rock.

Sir George Ripley, an English alchemist of the later fifteenth century, writes:

> These stones must be kept . . . in a warm place, or at least dry, as you would keep sugar, because they are of so tender and oily substance as they are apt to dissolve in every moist place.[4]

Ripley introduces a radically unusual idea of what is left at the end: It is a condition of sweetness and tenderness, soothing like oil and, in another passage, "like wax," that is, quite malleable.

These characteristics find their way automatically into conventional descriptions of old people. "The old man's a soft touch." "What a sweet old lady!" "I dissolve into tears over the silliest things." "I have a tender spot for that particular grandchild." "He's so slippery now, and goes whichever way you push him." "She's lost her edge; not so bitter anymore." In place of tough, sharp and flinty; easy, gentle, and loose.

French psychiatry of the nineteenth century attributed the aging character to "softening of the brain," an idea that influenced American medicine and popular notions of dementia. Where pathologists then saw softness inside the skull of the cadaver, today they find shrinking. These pathologies express two different kinds of anxieties about the old mind. In a century of hardheaded positive reason, softening meant madness and death; in times of grandiose titanic expansionism, we fear smallness. The same lesson can be learned regardless of the century: what we find as fact in the body is often prepared for, if not predicted, by imagination.

In his later years the Connecticut poet Wallace Stevens reflected upon George Santayana's last years in Rome in a convent with "No more than a bed, a chair and moving nuns." "How easily," says Stevens's poem, "the blown banners change to wings. . . . / The newsboys' muttering / Becomes another murmuring; the smell / Of medicine, a fragrantness." The philosopher exists "in two worlds" and the threshold between them softens. "On the threshold of heaven, the figures in the street / Become the figures of heaven. . . . Two parallels become one."[5]

Kathleen Woodward, the literary critic whose focus is the aging of writers, reflects on Stevens's reflections. She calls this movement from leaving to left a "transubstantiation." The process is a declension from three dimensions to two, from living existence to shadow substance, the being of an image. Only an image, nothing more than an image, yet altogether, and complete as, an image.

Ripley speaks of the philosopher's stone as "stones"—not one final result, a single thing made and done; rather, a little collection. You do not know which "you" will respond, who is at home, nor whether what is wanted today will be wanted by another "you" tomorrow. Call this condition disintegration, but also call it fullness of character expressing the complexity of its nature.

The plural nature of older age also helps account for the multitude of explanations of aging. Could any single theory account for all the stones? Some may age because of rapid metabolism, some because their cells have stopped dividing, some because their telomere strands are too long or too short or uncoordinated. Others may never have repaired the damage from earlier trauma; some may have duties to perform and must hang on at all costs; others live because God did not want them yet; still others have not come to their last astrological crisis—their thread not yet cut by the Lady of Fate. Then there are others who have still not left because of statistics— their geography, economics, occupation, and habits. I can imagine each stone having its particular story of how it became a stone and why it has lasted. One story does not fit all. Why should we lock ourselves into a unified theory of aging, or of character?

Our traits do not fit together; human nature is not a smooth amalgam. Imagine your eight great-grandparents all sitting down for dinner together. Could they find a common language, or share a dish they all could relish equally? Left at the end are unbridgeable gaps. In late years we are full of holes. Openings.

Openings? Rather, it seems that anyone reaching a certain age has a character encrusted with barnacles. How often we assume old people to be "unapproachable." Our ideas about them repel advances; we are biased against their looks, their smells, their idiosyncratic habits. Suppose, however, the tortoise's thicker, rougher appearance indicates that it's toughening its carapace to cover its inward softening, its gentled pride and yielding will. It is their softness that makes the old ones hard.

So Ripley's description of the pliable and tender condition of the achieved soul feels "unnatural"—or, as the alchemists said of the goal, an *opus contra naturam,* a work contrary to nature. A natural stone does not give way or shift its shape to accommodate what is pressed upon it. A waxy stone, however, yields to a warm hand and receives impressions easily. Just as easily, impressions are wiped away without a trace. Unlike hardened clay tablets and principles chiseled in stone, the philosophers' stone has a character malleable according to the occasion and the temperature; its precious quality is its moist tenderness.

Left at the end is not a simple piece of nature, but a peculiar concoction of soul and nature, a composition that is both psychologically susceptible and naturally resistant to being what it is not. We are able to receive, to be moved and touched, and yet we remain undeviatingly true to our given nature.

This softened character forms in the course of physical trials, which bring qualities of soul to clichés about natural decay. Being down-to-earth, hard-nosed, and sharp-eyed does not go far enough in the long run, and these qualities do not confirm uniqueness of character since they show the fortitude that everyone expects. The easy path of aging is to become a thick-skinned unbudging curmudgeon, an old buzzard, a battle-ax. To grow soft and sweet is the harder way.

Character is refined in the laboratory of aging. You don't get it right the first time. Each day brings another opportunity to strike the right mix, neither too malleable nor too rigid, neither too sweet nor too dry, giving the older character its power to bless with a tough-minded tenderness.

A story is told of the legendary philosopher Democritus. At 109 he began relinquishing the pleasures of life one by one by omitting an item of food from his diet each day. At the last, he had only a pot of honey left. He absorbed its sweet aromatic fragrance and passed away.

CHAPTER 18

Character Philosophized

Character died in the twentieth century. To revive it will not be easy. It had been drained of vitality centuries earlier, when it became irrelevant to the higher considerations of philosophy and science. Neither the laws that govern nature nor the principles grounding the human mind require an idea of character. It has been shoved aside into moral theology, social ethics, personal psychology, and the upbringing of children.

In its place a bevy of substitutes appeared: the will, the individual, the subject, the personality, the ego. Each is a way of speaking about a characterless, unified subjective agent. This Objective Observer is what we believe to be our center of consciousness. The substitutes for character come empty. They are deliberately abstract, whereas the old idea of character presented rich and recognizable traits, a crowd of qualities. Once the core of consciousness no longer included character, traits such as greed, zeal, combativeness, distractibility, punctiliousness . . . had to find a home elsewhere. They ended up in the twentieth-century unconscious as complexes attached to syndromes or as independent free-floating symptoms. More recently they have been tagged to genes.

The fall from top to bottom, the migration from center to

periphery accounts for the return of character to philosophy via psychoanalysis. There, character disorders and character analysis were never divorced from the nature of consciousness. Ego may be empty, but it is not alone; it is always crowded by and subject to the dynamics of character.

Norman Mailer once remarked, "Ego is the great word of the twentieth century." He was pointing to more than puffed-up, self-important vanity. He was remarking upon the emptiness concealed in the foundation of this period of history: Mr. Objective Observer. This characterless abstraction runs corporations, constructs the International Style of architecture, writes the language of official reports. He enforces the methods of scientific research, prefers systems to people, numbers to images. He defines the educational programs and the standards for testing them. He has also succeeded in separating the practices of law, science, medicine, and commerce from the character of the practitioner. He fosters the concocted names that rule diagnosis and the medicines that follow, and the acronyms of finance, institutions, and weaponry. This same characterless abstraction made possible the gulag and the KZ Lager. The one death that has caused so much death in the past century is the death of character.

———

The corpse invites an autopsy. It is hard, however, to isolate a single cause of death. Certainly, Schopenhauer's and Nietzsche's emphasis on the abstraction, "the will," as a force is one cause. Certainly another is the psychoanalytic notion of the ego as a purely functional agent, a kind of CEO or politician compromising between the rebellious left of demanding instincts and the moralistic right of handed-down dictates. Another cause of the death of character is a creator of characters, Henry James. Unlike novelists before him—Dickens, Tolstoy, Austen—he stays out of his own works; he is merely a hovering center of consciousness, an objective observer exposing the case as such.

Behind all these is the prime cause, still hiding out in the schools of Western philosophy: Kant's "transcendental unity of apperception." (As Kant said, the taste is not in the wine but in your apperception.) We are left with the faceless functionalism of pure consciousness, "sans teeth, sans eyes, sans taste, sans everything."

The idea of consciousness above all phenomena and attached to none provides the philosophical underpinnings for the Objective Observer in science, the objective narrator in literature, and the compression of consciousness into ego in psychology. This cool, abstracted agent is the subject that observes the world, wills its acts upon the world, and is potentially interchangeable with any other subjectivity anywhere (being transcendental, it is placeless and timeless). True consciousness is pure consciousness, beyond qualitative character of any kind.

Purity is poverty. The purification of consciousness impoverishes perceptions of character. When character reigned, in the Renaissance, Rabelais, Boccaccio, Shakespeare, and many others invented flamboyant language to describe people. Our casual observations today betray our indifference. Their characters do not draw our attention. What people *do* is who they are, is all they are. We see each other and treat each other as functions. What do we closely notice when we describe persons as "interesting," "deep," "creative," "awesome," "attractive," "strong," or "great," or when we pass them off as "weird," "oddball," "nerdy," "needy," "bitchy," "airhead," or "asshole"? These conventions of communication are hardly accurate images of character. Out of the shambles of abstraction that has placed emptiness in the center of humans as their consciousness, character must be born again.

Current deficiencies of character, both as an idea and in behavior, result from epistemology, the study of how we know. If the character of the knower is irrelevant to knowing, or even interferes with truest knowing, then character does not belong within philosophy's purview. Then knowledge and the methods of gaining knowledge can proceed unhampered by the character of the knower and by issues of value that are inescapably implied by the idea of character. Result: knowledge without value; valueless knowledge, which is euphemistically dubbed "objectivity."

When philosophy ignores the relevance of character for the value of knowledge, moral decline follows, and moral resurrection depends on philosophical correction. The righteous and the right who complain of moral decline in society look to "the family" for cause and cure. They should perform their postmortems more incisively. Then they would take their laments to philosophy and cut the overburdened, guilt-plagued families some slack.

The epistemological fault, in brief, is this. To know the world "out there," philosophy constructed a knowing subject "in here." As the world was conceived to be, ultimately, a characterless abstraction of space, time, and motion, so the knower had to be equally transcendent and objectified, that is, shorn of characteristics. The method of knowing the world had to be purified; otherwise our human observations would be all-too-human, qualified by individual subjectivity, merely anecdotal, therefore unreliable, therefore untrue. The ideal human as knower of truth must be a vacant mirror of purified consciousness.

Some thinkers would discard "consciousness" altogether. They call it the ghost in the machine; they assert that the relation between consciousness and brain is an insoluble problem, or that the problem results from the wrong question. They are right—so long as consciousness is undefiled by qualities, a sheer abstraction. To conceive of consciousness as energy aware of itself makes matters worse. It defines the one abstraction by means of three others: energy, awareness, and self.

To deconstruct this characterless, senseless world without color, taste, or sound means letting it decompose into its multitudinous qualities. It means taking the world as it is, a cornucopia of phenomena, and saving the phenomena from abstractions. Nature does indeed abhor a vacuum. A world defined by its qualities and perceived as qualities requires the same richness of its observers. Like knows like. If the world is a messy many, then the definition of consciousness follows one proposed early in the twentieth century by the French philosopher Henri Bergson: "qualitative multiplicity."

The knower becomes a bundle of traits and capacities, the ability to abstract merely one among many equally valuable potentials. The inmost nature of this knower, character, could no longer be contained within a single central core. It, too, would be imagined as an interplay of many characteristics. Consciousness would no longer be conceived as a clear light hovering over the face of the deep, observing each thing in its kind. Rather, the light would fracture, fluctuate, show variegations that reflect the characteristics of the world, our consciousness replying to its character. We would conceive of consciousness to be as multitudinous as the world, a microcosm of the macrocosm: as without, so within.

Rather than made in the image of a single transcendent God, we would imagine ourselves made like the multiple images of the world.

As we age, the world's character becomes more present to us, its "wonders never cease." Late consciousness that dims and blazes, comes and goes, corresponds with the world's pulsating diversity. The sun never stands still, and its light does not fall on all alike. True insight is through a glass darkly into the amazing difference of things, each one uniquely shadowed with the lines of its character.

—

What would happen were character to return *philosophically*? Speaking would radically change, because it would tell about ourselves and the world as we appear. Characteristics need descriptions, faces are particular, phenomena present images. Language can respond by speaking more descriptively, imagistically.

Since consciousness is always characterized, so is unconsciousness. It, too, would be qualified, no longer a generalized defense for rude and stupid acts, another mask of innocence. We would be ignorant, forgetful, cruel, arbitrary, enraged, careless, forgetful, foolish, sudden—but not "unconscious."

Rather than "the will" as an abstract component of a person and "to will" as a verb in varying strengths, we would speak of acting willfully, willingly, unwillingly, or hesitatingly, deliberately, aggressively ... "To think" would dissolve into the many modes of deliberation—unthinking, mindful, considered, thoughtless. Thought would never travel alone; it would always be qualified by companion adjectives such as "dark," "clear," "sharp," "tangled," "rigorous," "encompassing," "brilliant," "muddled," "logical," "incisive". ... Pure thought, too, would submit to further characterization.

We would name mental activities as do many indigenous languages and young children. We would speak of persons and places, divine or natural forces not with single abstractions, but always with descriptive adjectives, adverbs, and prepositional combinations: Sitting Bull, the Cat in the Hat, Aphrodite Kallipygos, Whiteness-Spreads-Out-Descending-to-Water (an Apache place name).

We would begin to see again what we saw before abstractions claimed our minds: Life as lived is completely characterized. Adjectives and adverbs are the actual forces at work in perceiving the world and in our behavior. Our speech would return to a correspondence with the world, which does not show a sheer unqualified cloud, a shrub, a mouse, but each cloud shaped, still or moving, related to the land below and to other clouds; each shrub a species and one of a kind; that particular mouse doing its thing in its singular way. Language would be creatively imagined to equal the imagination of the creation. I draw on a concise exposition of this style from the anthropologist Keith Basso:

> Thinking occurs in the form of "pictures" ... speaking involves the use of language to "depict" and "convey" these images to the members of an audience, such that they, on "hearing" and "holding" the speaker's words, can "view" the images in their own minds. Thinking, as Apaches conceive of it, consists in picturing to oneself and attending privately to the pictures. ... Apache hearers must always "add on" to ... these spoken images with images they fashion for themselves. This process is commonly likened to adding stones to a partially finished wall, or laying bricks upon the foundation of a house.[1]

Unlike abstract definitions, which settle language, conversations characterized by images are more like "projects to complete, invitations to exercise the imagination," Basso says.[2] Exercising imagination is also an invitation to continue the conversation by contributing rather than by adversarial opining. Inventing images while conversing is certainly more pleasurable than communicating information.

Roundabout slowness may be more accurately informative. Imagistic communication can be more economical in the long run than abstractions, which always demand further specifications. "She's a good mother," "a hard worker," "a loyal friend" are far too general to communicate definite information. The French anthropologist Lucien Lévy-Bruhl writes: "The most salient characteristic of most of the languages of the North American Indians is the care they take to express concrete details which our languages leave understood or unexpressed." He gives this example:

> A Ponka Indian in saying that man killed a rabbit, would have to say: the man, he, one, animate, standing, purposely killed by shooting an arrow the rabbit, he, the one, animal, sitting; for the form of the verb to kill would have to be selected, and the verb changes its form by inflection or to denote person, number, and gender (as animate or inanimate). . . . The form of the verb would also express whether the killing was done accidentally or purposely, and whether it was by shooting . . . and if by shooting, whether by bow and arrow, or by gun.[3]

Every inch characterized.

Contemporary culture, whose consciousness is defined by abstraction, looks down on peoples who speak this way. Less than fifty years ago they were referred to as "primitives." Abnormal psychology still considers this depictive, characterized speech diagnostic of circumstantiality and concretism. Certainly, communication is slowed. You, too, must be slow, if you say where you live by depicting your house and street rather than stating its name and number, even if the name is utterly generic—Lincoln or Maple or Main—and the number like millions of other similar numbers on houses. We hurry people to "get on with it," "spare me the details," "get to the point." We wean children from characterization toward abstraction and consider this step a measure of intelligence. All the while, we miss the world as it is and the complexity of our characters as they act in the world, a complexity that shows in just how we shoot the rabbit.

The philosophical upshot? In the telling of shooting the rabbit, consciousness and character coalesce. Hunter, rabbit, instrument, posture, intention compress into an instant of time, an image. Conscious precision characterizes every bit of the image: how rabbit freezes, how hunter pauses, how arrow flies and rabbit falls.

CHAPTER 19

The Character of Virtues,
or Character Moralized

Excluded from the high halls of science and philosophy, the study of character took up quarters among moralists, and the idea of character suffered from their influence. All the varieties of character were sorted into two bags: Good and Bad. The subject of character also degenerated. Once worthy of mature thought, it became a topic of simplistic instruction for good boys and girls.

Originally, character was not bent to fit moral strictures. The first "characterologists" spoke in images. They invented fictive figures and they observed life with a keen eye and witty tongue, like novelists and humorists today. The first book on the subject, *Characters,* by the successor of Aristotle at his school, Theophrastus of Lesbos (ca. 371–ca. 287 B.C.E.), portrays a series of imaginary figures that might have been drawn from the files of Central Casting: Petty Pride, Grumbling, Flattery, Loquacity, Tactlessness, Cowardice, Stupidity, Backbiting. Thirty in all. These are not condemned, nor are virtues like Sincerity, Grace, Honesty, Generosity described. Theophrastus' sketches serve more as a guidebook for street smarts and wising up to life, or for playing parts in stock comedy, than for raising children to be virtuous. He never tells you it is bad to be mean; he is content to portray Meanness as it appears:

> when he entertains friends to a feast, not to set enough bread before them; to borrow of a stranger that is staying in his house; to say as he carves the meat that the carver deserves a double portion; and when he is selling his wine, to sell it watered to his friend.

So with Nastiness:

> to blow his nose at table; to bite his nails when he is sacrificing with you; to spit when he is talking with you . . . to hiccup in your face. He will go to bed with his wife with hands unwashed and his shoes on.

Classical writers like Plutarch and Suetonius studied the lives of eminent men and observed their strengths and weaknesses, but only in Christian times was character heavily moralized. Biblical types became exemplary figures: Ruth, the loyal follower; Abraham, the obedient patriarch; Aaron, the brother; Martha, Peter, Judas . . . The saints presented images for emulation and for prayer to gain the virtue personified by the saint. During the Renaissance, Machiavelli and Pico della Mirandola and other students of character returned to the classical style. Their passion was more psychological than moral, more about how we are on earth than how we should be for heaven.

The Victorians thoroughly moralized character. As profit and loss, fame and failure are the poles of our contemporary compass, so virtue and vice were theirs. Their compass lay inside character, pulling it apart, making it a battleground where "the good fight" had to be fought. The American "War Between the States" intensified the interior conflict, reenforcing with martial values the virtues of self-reliant Protestantism. Character was the province of moralists, the Will writ large, and manly men: Francis Parkman, Oliver Wendell Holmes, Jr., Emerson, and lastly reformer Theodore Roosevelt, who proclaimed the vigorous idea of character from the political platform.

Emerson begins his essay "Character" with four paragraphs on morals, three of them opening with that very word. "The will constitutes the man," he writes. In this Emerson is little different from the most influential of all Victorian philosophers, John Stuart Mill: "A character is a completely fashioned will." How is this will fashioned? Through habit, which William James explains in his *Talks to Teachers* (1899). The will develops the habit of habits. "Keep the faculty of effort alive in you by a little gratuitous exercise every day."[1] "We must make automatic and habitual, as early as possible, as many useful actions as we can."[2]

This line comes around again with William Bennett, who often draws his material for the education of character from works of "around the turn of the twentieth century." Children develop "good habits . . . through repeated practices." Virtues must be instilled because "children are not born with this knowledge."[3]

Moralist admonitions aim at youth. "As early as possible," writes William James. Character moralized omits the late years, when the body breaks the habits of conformity and character comes through the cracks. Moralized character has nothing to say about aging, nor does aging have anything to say about character other than expostulations to youth about going wrong. For old explorers embarking for foreign shores, virtuous Victorian platitudes could not be more irrelevant.

The moralization of character is not just past history. The phrase "character issue" refers to habits decried from the pulpit and by prissy politicians, rather than to the basic meaning of "character": the particular marks of identity that make one person different from another. "Character" in America still implies definite Victorian virtues: backbone, not taste buds; fist, not soul. Character certainly has no locus below the belt.

In keeping with a characteristically American priority—judgment before curiosity—we still declare a phenomenon good or bad before we become interested in it. This shelters our innocence from deeper engagement. We have good dreams and bad; she's a good kid, he's bad. Enough said. A Puritan's black hat hangs in every American hallway. Praise or blame reinforces the moral idea of character, and making this judgment also makes decisively clear the virtuous morality of our own character.

Character had a better refuge, its oldest, one well outside the military school, the pulpit, and the orphanage: astrology, where it still thrives today. The popular vitality of astrology attests to the need for a psychology of character for the conduct of life.

Astrology offers a language of traits. It can be caught in the traps of pseudoscientific reckoning in numbers and be leveled down to the practical ego's demands for winning success, finding love, and avoiding trouble. Astrology's main virtue, however, is the presentation of a heavenful of characteristics that refer the individual soul to archetypal powers. Its mythical imagination connects habitual tendencies to profounder necessities. It speaks of character in images.

If your pattern shows lots of elemental water, with the Fish especially dominant, your character may tend toward dissolution and deep, if cool, affinities. You might be sensitive to the slightest waves in the surroundings and find it hard to awaken from nightly dreams. You would avoid irrevocable decisions in favor of fluctuating ambivalence, and you would enjoy big storms and sucking tides, for you can thrive in the invisible currents under water.

This can all be said without a word of moral remonstrance. No blame. The pattern does not predict that you will become a drunk, a nurse, a tardy procrastinator, a romantic violinist, a suffering masochist, an intuitive art dealer, or a gumshoe detective attuned to hidden vibes. No program for moral improvement; it just offers metaphoric insights, so that one's character be lived more intelligently. Astrology's reading of character uses a subtle imagistic language; moralized character needs little more than "good" and "bad."

Biology is opening another route into the morality of character. Rather than assuming that eternal verities come from revealed religion or from inculcation through centuries of tradition, today science searches for the genetics of moral sentiments. The eminent biologist E. O. Wilson proposes an empirical attack on the mystery of morality. He says we need to measure the heritability of ethical behavior, and identify the prescribing genes.

To the more basic question "Why do moral sentiments exist in the first place?" Wilson answers: "Presumably they contributed to the survival and reproductive success during long periods of prehistoric time in which they genetically evolved."[4]

Morals' value is in usefulness; Wilson's position is utilitarian. These ethics would have to say that compassion, generosity, friendship, and other virtues are good because presumably they served evolution. From a different vantage point, character traits are primarily required by the soul for its life, which cannot be satisfactorily lived without values, ideals, and moral dilemmas. If moral virtues are at all useful they are useful for the character of the individual; their value, however, lies not in their usefulness now or millions of years ago, but in the style of their enactment.

———

How different the approach to character in these pages! We are trying to free it from both religion and science by deepening its psychology, finding character defined less by moral virtues than by individual oddities. These traits may often be unsuitable to the programs of religion and unserviceable to the genes' survival, yet they may further the imaginative richness of life.

My emphasis on character as images revealed in traits continues the classical tradition from Theophrastus into Renaissance character descriptions written, painted, symbolized. Moral virtues make up only a part of these descriptions and only some of the content of character.

More important than the amount and strength of any other content is that of imaginative intelligence once called perspicacity or providence. It is a kind of insight, an intuitive sense of the images at work in one's life. These are one's actual truth. "Truth" not as doctrine or principle; truth as instinct. For character acts as an underlying instinct, incisively underlining the moves we make, the words we say, marking their style. It is an imagining force, and we need imaginative intelligence to track its marks.

There is an intuitive feeling that keeps humans from going too far off course or beyond our bounds, engaging in worlds that are inauthentic to our nature. This instinctive sense parallels similar limiting responses in all species, perhaps in all things, keeping them true to form. We humans can go a long way with what we each are. Our oddity may be our most enduring long-term asset, but we cannot add one inauthentic iota without incurring the collapse of supporting instinct and the wrath of the gods. The limiting effect of one's innate image prevents that inflation, that trespassing or hubris that the classical world considered the worst of human errors. In this way, character acts as a guiding force.

The instinctual limitation may appear in the still, small voice of conscience, as an inhibiting symptom, or as a moral principle conceived as duty, perseverance, law-abiding honesty. It shows up early in life giving the smallest child the voice to say that first adamant and unbudging "No!"

Here we must remember that character is always qualified. It consists in traits, images, qualities. By definition, character refers to the distinguishing marks that make a thing recognizably different from every other thing. Each character is held to itself by the qualities peculiar to it. It is necessarily limited by its own qualifications. A "bad" character could refer only to an utterly empty one, a person with no distinguishing characteristics whatsoever, innocent of qualities, a blank. If sins are your only qualities, you may be without morals, but not without character.

Therefore, a person of character will not necessarily be a moral exemplar. Nor will a bundle of reprehensible sins define a bad character. A bad character would refer to a person with little insight, adrift among events, clinging to stiff virtues but unanchored in his or her own image, without an inkling of his uniqueness. A bad character is simply one who does not imagine who he is—in short, an innocent. That he is disloyal, shameless, irresponsible, untrustworthy, dissolute are all flaws that flow from the first. Innocence has no guiding governance but ignorance and denial.

I am here following a tradition that begins with Socrates, who considered ignorance, especially ignorance of soul, to be evil, and dedication to enlightenment to be the primary calling of human beings. The tradition insists that a "good" character requires a psychological education, which is nothing more than the dispelling of innocence. It is a work in the shadows. Socrates and Freud labored in the same cave.

I differ from them inasmuch as their path of insight is ana-lytical, mine imaginative. You do not *know* yourself; you dis-cover yourself. You catch a glimpse, recognize a characteristic response, a preference. You see the consistency of your image despite the ups and downs of mood. And you need others to wake you up if you're to find your face. Self-knowledge appears and disappears as insights in the play of life.

Since a differentiated intelligence about one's character takes a lifetime, education of character cannot be accomplished in younger years. Good habits may start well, but in time they turn to rusty chains, shackling character's instinctive advance. In youth we may be morally trained and may be taught lessons about character, but only the matured imagination can confirm the learning. Whether early or late, shame, guilt, and low self-esteem are necessary to character formation because they eat away at innocence.

Shame is one of the "gifts reserved for age," according to Eliot. He goes on to describe shame as

> . . . the rending pain of re-enactment
>   Of all that you have done, and been; the shame
>   Of motives late revealed, and the awareness
> Of things ill done and done to others' harm
>   Which once you took for exercise of virtue.[5]

Self-delusion is the mask of innocence in old age, much as innocence covers itself with denial earlier on. Shame which can make the body blush and writhe, confirms character's instinc-tive abhorrence of innocence.

We give honorable names to the governance of instinct. We say, "It is beneath my dignity"; "It is a matter of self-respect"; "My pride would not let me do that." We decline a tempting offer with noble discourse, whereas more likely what holds us back is fear of going beyond our limits, betraying our instinct, and being left by the gods.

If we do not stop thinking of character as a function of will, if we do not locate character in the instinctual soul, then we go on exhorting ourselves to do better, try harder, like marines in boot camp, innocent of one of the psyche's basic truths: the taller the tree, the greater its shadow. Good habits cannot prevent bad falls.

—

Here arises the moral mistake. Ethics is not something one puts into character, inoculating it against sin and bolstering its immunity to temptations. Morality so conceived is merely a packet of goods bought by the will and practiced as a habit. Even the habit of habits cannot save us from the unsavory traits of character. Suppression of the undesirable goes only so far and lasts only so long; then the repressed returns with a vengeance.

This universal lesson comes not only from Freud. The lasting strength of the immoral and amoral is taught by the world's history and its literature. From De Sade and Dostoevsky through Sinclair Lewis and Sherwood Anderson to *Peyton Place* and *Dallas* we receive a common message: The shadow knows as much about the soul as any "book of virtues." The ten listed by William Bennett read as if written by tough-minded men of the past century, before the soul's cellar was reopened by Baudelaire, Marx, Nietzsche, Freud, and the First World War, which said good-bye to all that. Character conceived in the nineteenth-century style is unwounded by history; it reeks of sanctimoniousness. What it promotes is regressive, repressive, sentimental, and fundamentally wrongheaded, because its good intentions pave over the rending dilemmas of post-Hitlerian morality.

Ethics emerges from character not as virtue or vice, but as

each character's particularity, and peculiarity. Each character brings along its bundle of values and traits—and the lasting strength of the unserviceable. Cain outlasted Abel, and Mr. Hyde is as enduring as Dr. Jekyll. As character embraces both good and evil, it is beyond both. Its integrity is merely the pattern of its strung-together parts, even if that pattern is as tension-ridden and duplicitous as Jekyll and Hyde.

The moral idea of character prevents us from seeing character. We see morals. Since a teenage kid has blond hair, lives at home, and has no juvenile record, we see no further. Since Hitler had ideals for his nation, enacted the protocols and signed treaties, other leaders of the time saw no further. Michael Milken, Ivan Boesky, J. Edgar Hoover, and Edwin Meese held responsible jobs, requiring resourcefulness and self-discipline. Their characters were not further examined—until Mr. Hyde emerged. A society that promotes Dr. Jekylls through books of virtue may actually be fostering Mr. Hydes.

Some of what I mean by "*force* of character" is the persistence of the incorrigible anomalies, those traits you can't fix, can't hide, and can't accept. Resolutions, therapy, conversion, the heart's contrition in old age—nothing prevails against them, not even prayer. We are left realizing that character is indeed a force that cannot succumb to willpower or be reached by grace. The force of its flaws mocks all the virtuous books, whose efforts to enlighten are candles in the wind.

We can reconceive the whole business of character by focusing less on children and what they should know than on old age and what we do know. I am compelled and constrained by what I do not control. Character forces me to encounter each event in my peculiar style. It forces me to differ. I walk through life oddly. No one else walks as I do, and this is my courage, my dignity, my integrity, my morality, and my ruin.

CHAPTER 20

Character Imagined

The idea of "image" has threaded its way throughout this book. I have claimed that people are formed into images and age progressively into their images. Memories of them are as much products of imagination as deposits of fact. We saw the dissolution into image in a passage from Gide. We saw Jung merging into images of nature, "plants, animals, clouds," while his image endures in the imagination of his public. The story of the woman driving off, leaving a lasting image, provided another example. All that we discovered about the face further reinforced the thesis that character and image are inseparable.

Although our memory images of people's characters are as much products of imagination as deposits of fact, this does not mean that our images are purely personal fantasies and that imagination is a function inside each privately enclosed skull. I do not consider imagination to be a mental faculty only.

Here, I follow the Romantics, who took the power of imagination right out of the head and into the cosmos. "Jesus, the Imagination," exclaimed Blake, by which he meant the cosmic creative force of the world soul, or *anima mundi,* which produces the images that we perceive—and receive. Images come to us, in reverie, in dreams, in sudden clear insights, and during the long struggles of careful thought. They come to us from the world's imagination, with which ours corresponds and, according even to such skeptics and rationalists as Hume and Kant, on which our understanding of the world depends. "Without Imagination we should have no knowledge whatsoever, but we are scarcely ever conscious [of this]," said Immanuel Kant.

Because consciousness has become identified with the sense of sight, "to see an image" has come to refer to an optical experience. Images have been conceived as visual representations, rather than as presentations of significance, or even as presences. As we feel feelings, sense sensations, think thoughts, so we imagine images. We do not have to see them *literally*. We do not literally see the images in poems or the characters in novels, or even those in paintings. We "see" images with imagination, and that is how we see character, too. It is like the presence of a person.

To train the eye to see imaginatively we could not do worse than take university courses in psychology, or approach with a diagnostic manual those oddities called abnormal. The study of character does not appear in the curriculum of psychology; more appropriate methods of study go on in other departments—film, theater, literature, biography, political science, military history, and art history—and in law, because the courts still call character witnesses to testify. To improve the faculty of imagination, we must go where we are encouraged to practice imagining.

More than a faculty, imagination is also one of the great archetypal principles, like love, order, beauty, justice, time. We sense these principles coursing through us and even hold their reins in our hands. Yet they are also beyond us and never in our hands. We do not put beauty or love or order in the world. We find them there, and we respond to them as smaller correspondents of these larger powers.

So, too, imagination. It endlessly produces possibilities, which our imagining capability receives and elaborates. We make small human versions of order, measure out time, construct things of beauty, codify justice, and demonstrate love. All the while, we know that justice and beauty and love are never fully captured by the corresponding human institutions. Why shouldn't the same be true of imagination? As we cannot command love, or produce beauty without the aid of luck or inspiration, so we cannot bring imagination to heel. Fantasies are more like the spirit. They blow where they will, and we are lucky if one comes near enough and lasts long enough to grasp.

We are part and parcel of the world. Our bodies share its carbon, oxygen, and salt water, and we also participate as images in its imagination. Although the elements are formulated into numbers and acronyms like CO_2 and H_2O, they contain a rich symbolic imagery. The French physicist, chemist, and philosopher of imagination Gaston Bachelard showed in book after book how imagery forms our thinking about elemental nature, although, as Kant said, "we are scarcely ever conscious" of this.

Our bodies are both anatomical and imaginative structures. What is left at the end are the bones of the body and the lines of character that form images, or that images have formed. We are like materialized poems capable of intense exhilaration and suffering. This imaginative body is the stuff of dance and sculpture, and impels the rhythms of oratory, music, and writing.

Every breath we take, we take from the cosmos. We inhale its air; we speak with its breath; its pneuma is our inspiration. "Cosmos" indicates a world formed by aesthetics. "Cosmetics," derived from *kosmos,* gives the clue to the early meanings of the Greek word, when it was linked with the dress of women, with decoration and embellishment, with all things fitting, in order, furnished, and arranged, and with ethical implications of appropriateness, decency, honor. The aesthetic imagination is the primary mode of knowing the cosmos, and aesthetic language the most fitting way to formulate the world.

Characteristics last as images. Great-grandfather in his huge, old restaurant kitchen at daybreak, unkempt, slippered, night-shirted, prying into leftovers. What's been stolen; what's been wasted. Great-grandmother's jutting jaw, darting eyes and piercing glance. She may have lost her mind, but not her wit; lost her balance, but not her thrust. These traits become independent variables, coming and going. They flash back as images the older one gets. The individuality of the person becomes a shifting kaleidoscope, each of us becoming more unique, instable and complex. It is a conclusion from research that "with increasing age there is increasing variation among individuals."[1]

"Late-stage thinking is complex," concludes another investigator of aging.[2] It is complex because it is imaginative—metaphoric, multileveled, suggestive. It harbors a different kind of intelligence than the brightness of youth and the judicious pragmatics of middle age. To borrow a phrase from Robert Bly: "The image is a form of intelligence."

I can imagine a purpose for the complexity of late-stage thinking: A new and necessary intelligence is forming. Hades, the mythical god of the underworld, where souls go after life and continue to exist as images, was described by Socrates (in *Cratylus*) as having the finest intelligence. This, Socrates explains, is why souls do not come back. In the company of Hades, their greatest desire is fulfilled: endless intelligent philosophizing in a world wholly composed of images.

If the character of a person is a complexity of images, then to know you I must imagine you, absorb your images. To stay connected with you, I must stay imaginatively interested, not in the process of our relationship or in my feelings for you, but in my imaginings of you. The connection through imagination yields an extraordinary closeness. Where imagination focuses intently on the character of the other—as it does between opposing generals, guard and hostage, analyst and patient—love follows.

The human connection may benefit from exhortations to love one another, but for a relationship to stay alive, love alone is not enough. Without imagination, love stales into sentiment, duty, boredom. Relationships fail not because we have stopped loving but because we first stopped imagining.

CHAPTER 21

Grand Parenting

How to be a good parent? Guidance is easy to find on the self-help bookshelf. But what is *grand* parenting, and how does one move from parenting to something grander?

To answer this question is to take on the question posed at the beginning of this book: "Why do we live so long—especially women, who may go on for fifty years beyond their fertility cycles?" The selfish gene theory puts the egg before the chicken because "the sole activity and telos of genes is to create conditions for their own reproduction."[1] Eggs use chickens to produce new eggs. Why does this theory not get rid of us, once we are out of eggs? How account for the endurance of tough old birds?

The endurance of older women signifies more for propagation of the human species than carrying viable eggs and birthing babies. As Moscow grandmothers stood in front of Russian tanks and stopped them cold, could a "grandmother hypothesis" stop the flattening steamroller of genetic reductionism?

Elderly women add to culture and help perpetuate the species by caring for the young, relieving pregnant and lactating mothers. Their care serves to reduce infant mortality, although they themselves may be infertile. "Grandmothers empowered the human species to become the planet's dominant animal," writes Theodore Roszak in his exposition of the "grandmother hypothesis."[2] They also carry cultural knowledge.

We may imagine elderly ladies void of ova but packed with memes. Memes are the cultural equivalent of genes. Like genes they are independent of their carriers. They transmit bits of culture from generation to generation. Daniel Dennett describes them: They are deposited in cultural artifacts like "pictures, books, sayings," "as complex ideas that form themselves into *distinct memorable units*" (italics in source). "A meme's existence depends on a physical embodiment in some medium."[3] Why not grandparents as that embodiment, that medium?

Grandmothers and grandfathers maintain rituals and traditions, possess a hoard of primal stories, teach the young, and nurture the memory of the ancestral spirits who guard the community. Grandparents listen to dreams, and tell you what a new word means; they can tie a fly, bait a hook, and know where the best place is. They live among odd objects, which they cherish, and smells unforgettable. They have little time left, yet so much time to spare.

The intricate, subtle process that slowly makes soul in a human being—the hands-on knowledge of nature and of the street, of dreams, skills, manners, and tastes, and of what happened before now and long, long ago—requires the intelligence of elders who devote themselves to other ends than pragmatic functioning. Their days of hunting and gathering, childbearing and nursing are past, yet their days continue because they have equally important duties: culture.

I would add only this to Roszak's grandmother hypothesis. Grandparenting begins in the character of the older person who has an eye on the character of the young ones and searches for their grander possibilities. A grandparent can afford visions grander than the difficult and dutiful routines of the parents. The old man's eyes may be clouded but his vision may see clearly, partly because he is close to the child's affection. In many indigenous societies, the deeper instructive and affective connections skip a generation. Since both grandparents and grandchildren are partly marginalized, the young fantast joins the old eccentric against a common opponent, the adult generation between them.

The grandparent who has little culture "backward" can hardly carry culture forward. He may dispossess himself of his things as he ages, but he may not put down the baggage of knowledge and history. This knowledge and history cannot be found in books or viewed on a screen. It must be personified, spoken in words that are no longer current, displayed in styles no longer fashionable, present in faces that cannot dissemble. Elders are like living memes, units of cultural heredity, which make, in Roszak's words, "higher evolution possible."[4]

Grandparents need grander ideas, especially about their evolutionary roles. Altruism supports the grander parenting that can motivate elders. "Higher evolution" can imagine the whole world as a servicing organism tacitly maintained by human decency.

It is unseemly for a mature person who would mentor others and foster civilization's future to hold to simplistic geneticism—to believe that we are each directed by our genes and that their self-perpetuation is the origin of even our altruistic acts. That theory discounts generosity, conceiving it to be indirectly promoting the species' gene pool. It discounts our wish for the welfare of others, including the conservation of nature and the preservation of history. It makes of self-sacrifice merely the selfish gene's manipulation in aid of its own survival. Psychopaths think this way too, which to my elderly mind means that the selfish gene theory, even while it promotes evolution, gives authoritative backing to the selfish individualism of psychopathy, and is, in effect, a psychopathic idea.

Because grandparents have little time left, they generally relish this world and its beauty. Yet they have one foot in another world; they can see the angel in the child, and its calling. They can imagine the child beyond its childhood. Even if this insight becomes tetchy and opinionated, the *idea* behind the insight is precious, for it affirms the reality of angel, calling, character, destiny lifting the child from his toys to the skies. Inspiration also belongs to grandparenting.

Worrying doesn't. The worst we can do is worry. It is more insidiously toxic than scolding for faults or demanding for success. Worry does nothing for the child except to make its life, all life, uncertain. Behind the "grandmother hypothesis" are the mythical grandmothers Cybele, Gaia, Rhea, Isis, Nut, guarantors of this earth and the whole wide world. A hymn to Cybele addresses her as "mother of all that exists"; Gaia is the "foundation of all," "the oldest one."[5] Nut, as the sheltering sky, extends her arms over all the earth. Rhea, the grandmother of Dionysos, put his dismembered parts together and brought him back to life. The grandmother of Jesus, St. Anne, older than Mary, Queen of Heaven, has as her emblem a door. Grandmother herself may be a shut-in, but through her the world opens out safely. Though not blindly. A hymn to Rhea calls her "deceitful savior." She was savvy to the darker side of things and thus could protect one from them.

The mythical grandmothers give grounding. They provide footholds for the first adventurous steps, and they are permanent, indestructible, and absolute in their giving. Grandparenting inoculates the child against paranoia. The very way an old lady crosses the street or talks with a stranger shows that confidence, demonstrating to younger persons that they can step forward without worry. It is like an animal faith, an instinctive reliance on the world. The sky will not fall in, the ground underfoot not give way. It shows faith in the child's ability to find its way, rather than hope that the child will realize your investment. Grandparenting says, "Yes, you belong here; the world has place after place where you may stand and be well. Don't worry—but don't be stupid, either."

We impede evolution and the development of the human species if we neglect the aged. This we will do until we recognize that their character can shelter civilization from its own predatory frenzy. This is Roszak's thought, in my words. It is not merely a defense of the old by two old men of the same generation, but a defense of the values of civilization against the destructive force and narrowed imagination of genetic engineering, hog-wild capitalism, technocratic government, and the salvational fundamentalism that would leap over the beauty of this world in a rush to the next. What is left when we old ones have left is that beauty, the younger generations' inheritance. Before we leave, we need to uphold our side of the compact of mutual support between human being and the being of the planet, giving back what we have taken, securing its lasting beyond our own.

CHAPTER 22

The Old Scold

Because one function of grandparenting has so fallen out of fashion, I feel compelled to single it out. Like cracking a ruler across the schoolboy's knuckles and washing the young girl's mouth out with soap (for lying or dirty language), severe dressings-down by old scolds have become only a miserable memory.

Well, not altogether. An old scold appeared in a small tour group I joined in Greece some years ago. Most of the tourists were Americans, a few Europeans. One woman, turning forty, laughed too often, too hysterically. She smiled at everyone in the group and out, connecting all around wherever we traipsed in the rocky, reticent, and sacred terrain. She called herself Debbie.

The oldest woman in the group, from French Switzerland, dressed Debbie down, and in front of some of the others. In essence she said: Debbie's laugh was too young; moreover, by now she should be using her full name, a beautiful name with biblical origins, Deborah.

The old scold—Madame Lafarge, let's call her—came from the city of John Calvin and seemed to be acting the censor in his name. Mme. Lafarge was rigid in her code, cool in her connection, and hostile in her style of reproof. She had a lesson to teach: A woman of forty is not a girl. She must consider what comes out of her mouth. She must be able to judge when to connect, with whom to smile, how to contain. Friendliness with everyone is not friendly, but inconsiderate. Such was the content of Madame's lesson.

For me, there were other lessons. Her intervention alone was one: An older person may risk being offensive in defense of important values—values that some of the other Americans did not perceive. They saw only a clash of cultures—the Swiss were puritan, the French nasty; Europeans are still basically snobs, superior. . . .

Although we were in Greece, these Americans did not glimpse a far older cultural clash, which has recurred in different ways throughout history. Mme. Lafarge's sense of manners came from something deeper than Miss Manners. At stake here was Athens against the Barbarians. Behind the old scold is civilization attempting to maintain civility. Mme. Lafarge must have been prompted by the corrective spirit of Athene herself, mother of civilization. No wonder we stood in awe of this small elderly lady's scolding: Athene has devastating power. No wonder Debbie folded.

I learned a second lesson. Mme. Lafarge took her personal irritation and ran with it. She might have held her tongue, accommodated herself to the group. She might have rationalized her annoyance as her fault, a result of her age, her digestion, her tiredness. Instead, she raised the level of her irritation from the trivial and personal to the cultural and important. She was protesting not merely manners, not merely an ethics of social behavior. Nor was she protesting Debbie's attention-demanding narcissism. It was as if Debbie had come to a grove of olive trees with a boom box and played the wrong music. Mme. Lafarge stood her senior ground and showed that part of that ground is aesthetic judgment. Fitness, appropriateness, sensitivity—aesthetic considerations belong as much to behavior as does finding the right word to keep the rhythm in a line of poetry.

Scolding is a poetic act: *"scold"* comes from *Skald,* Norse for poet. Early on, a scold was not a Calvinist but a ribald, noisy, quarreling woman. The scolding poet reproves the community. Like Jeremiah's, her scolding constantly warns and she is misunderstood like Cassandra. She is perceived as crazy, offensive; she disrupts communal harmony, so that a scold is commonly seen as a faultfinder who must wrangle her points to the end. The tacit complicity of the group with Debbie's style under the compact of harmonious equality drove Mme. Lafarge to her eccentric, disruptive rebuke. She became an old scold, as if having stepped back into the word itself.

One of the poet's tasks is to bring a community to its senses and wake it up, and to do this by aesthetic means that are hardly distinguishable from moral chiding. If the family code forbids cursing, blasphemy, and obscenity, a child who swears and blasphemes is punished for immorality. But if her language is unfitting to the occasion, if her behavior is insensitive, insulting, and self-indulgent, then her offense is aesthetic. Mme. Lafarge was aesthetically offended; Debbie had bad taste.

Was Mme. Lafarge in bad taste for shaming a woman who hadn't really done any harm? The older woman had not picked on Debbie's pigtails, her baggy clothes, her snacking habits, or her other idiosyncrasies. Aging was the issue, aging as essential to character—inauthentic in one means inauthentic in the other. To Mme. Lafarge Debbie was *essentially* inappropriate and therefore out of sync with the cosmos. Not to act one's age, not to *be* one's age, is so radical a fault that all others flow from it.

Later reflections on the incident brought home a third lesson, about authority. What had authorized this elderly, rather quiet and unassuming woman, who was not physically domineering (or even quite up to the pace of the tour), to come forward with such vigor? She was certainly a minority, with no support group. Yet, whether by Calvin, Athene, or civilization itself, she was authorized. She had authority, although she was powerless. Perhaps its source was simply her years. Had these years shown her the intelligence that lies in one's heartfelt emotions, and taught her that offenses which strike the heart are a call to demonstrate character? She did not deny the passion in her judgment, or avoid the risk of scolding even if everyone else in that little group might find her wrong.

And not everyone did. A young couple told me some days later how impressed they had been by this scolding. Debbie had been ruining their trip. Her habits had usurped their private evening conversations, which had turned to gossip instead of Greece. Instead of their secret bad-mouthing, Mme. Lafarge had issued a public scolding and put the whole group back on track. They admired her guts. She had done a real service.

As Debbie saw it, Mme. Lafarge was heartless. Moreover, what I am now calling authority, the psychologists among the Americans on the tour called a power struggle between generations. They saw two antagonists with equally justified opinions vying for competitive edge: Whose style would run the group? The content of the rebuke was incidental to them. The "problem" was a group dynamic, and Debbie's crumbling meant that she had low self-esteem. She could not stand up for herself.

After the reflections brought on by this book, I now understand what Debbie knew in her bones: Her personality had been defeated by the older woman's character.

In my imagination, Debbie has not forgotten this incident. It will last long after the old scold herself has passed to whatever reward she receives. I imagine Debbie will be passing on what she has learned; she may be mentoring others with a sudden tongue. We can all recall a drama coach, a music teacher, a shop supervisor, an old uncle coming down hard, boring in on our character with scorn and ridicule in the name of values that must be acknowledged, defended, and passed on. The scold as instrument of tradition: This is also grandparenting.

Grandparenting means parenting something grander than your own personal offspring. Opportunities to act like Mme. Lafarge are everywhere. Civilization is always at stake; barbarians are always at the gates, or in the high seats, cloaked in the robes of office.

CHAPTER 23

The Virtues of Character

Besides giving aging its value and its meaning, character has other virtues. We can lay these out quite succinctly, circumscribing the idea of character.

1. The idea of character depends on the archetypal notion of difference. Character is defined in the simplest dictionary form as "any observable mark, quality or property by which any thing, person, species or event may be known as *different* from something else" (italics mine).[1] Character thus confirms, even trumpets, the unique, the singular, the odd. Since character locates individuality in the observable marks of difference, eccentricity becomes necessary to character.

2. Bodily events are equally representative of character and may not be excluded from inquiry into the psychology of character. Character comprehends psyche and soma; character is a psychosomatic idea.

3. Character is presentational. It requires descriptive language—adjectives, such as "stingy," "sharp," "opinionated"; adverbs, such as "slowly," "carefully," "deliberately"—which transmits images and awakens feelings. "Go in fear of abstractions," wrote Ezra Pound, "use no adjective which does not reveal something." Character richly refurbishes psychological

discourse with the 17,953 trait names listed by the Harvard Psychological Laboratory. Each specifies a form of human behavior. In capturing character precisely and comprehensively, poetic speech far surpasses the language of behavioral science.

4. Character is a cluster of characteristics. A character is "not presumed to be strictly unified. . . . The character is the entire configuration without the traits seen as layers with a core holding them together," writes the philosopher Amélie Rorty.[2] Since the idea of character defies simplistic reductions, an inquiry into character calls for a complex kind of intelligence. It will appreciate the juxtaposition of layers as a poetic or painted image and it will abandon the search for a unifying core.

5. Character is perceptible as an image. It is on display as style, habit, gesture, disposition, constitution, carriage, mien, presence. The face reveals character and appeals to character. As image, character must be imagined as well as perceived.

6. Character has always been distinguished from talent, skill, gifts, and measurable abilities. It can be lamed by deficiencies and trapped in fixations, all the while talents and skills exhibit brilliance. Character does not yield to standardized measurements of performance. The characteristic uniqueness of a style eludes analysis.

7. Character also eludes the moral clamp. It reveals itself not in the morality of behavior but in its style. Character traits include vices and virtues. They do not define character. Character defines them. Perseverance or loyalty may instigate a criminal act as well as a just one. Friendship may motivate revenge as well as self-sacrifice. The imaginative scope of character cannot be pressed into an ethical definition without perverting its nature and sterilizing its fecundity.

8. Unlike "personality," character is impersonal. Rocks, paintings, houses, even kinds of bacteria and logical propositions demonstrate character. The discourse of personality is human psychology; of character, imaginative description.

9. As with personality, so with "self." Self is reflexive, pointing back to the subject, merging with its abstract rival, "ego." Selves narrow down to people. We do not speak of the self of a horse, a pine tree, or a promontory, yet we sense their definite

characters. Self, often equated with the timeless in a human being, has little to contribute to the archetypal issue of oldness. Obituaries speak of character traits, but would fall mute attempting to eulogize the deceased's self. Formulations of self are without limiting characteristics. Self conflates with God.

10. Uniqueness carries character beyond temperament and type. Type reduces character to two dimensions of "flat characters" (E. M. Forster's phrase). Temperament will manifest itself variously, depending on character. An introverted temperament may show innumerable styles: stubbornness, fearfulness, superficial adaptation, shyness, seclusion, systematic denial, deep concentration. These phrases call up images; "introvert" leaves one blank. While introversion requires a schema of contrasts for its definition, the traits and images of character stand on their own.

11. Character leaves traces in political history. As a determinant of the course of human events, character ties psychology to society, drawing psychology away from its obsessive subjectivity.

12. Character reintroduces Fate into psychology. Substitutions for character eliminated this ancient connection. "Ego," "personality," "self," "agent," "individual" reduce psychology to the study of human behavior—to processes, functions, motivations—and omit the fateful consequences implied by the idea of character. Psychology shorn of fate is too shallow to address its subject, the soul.

13. Character is to late years as individual calling of the daimon is to early years; it gives sense and purpose to the changes of aging. Character is a therapeutic idea.

CHAPTER 24

Finish

Let us imagine that we have followed the noblest saintly advice and that its aims have been accomplished. We have harnessed our rage, perfected our love, and given our will a moral direction. What question is left at the end? Have we still something to do? Or, do we let aging ravage us, *fiat mihi,* let it be done to me, apart from all efforts and all questionings, because aging puts a finish to character?

But—how does character put its finish on aging?

"Finished" means over and done with, as at the finish line in a horse race. "Finished" also means finely wrought, highly polished, like the sheen on worn, well-waxed wood. What is left after leaving is the actual state of character, the way the years have put a finish on it and not merely to it.

Finis was the Latin translation of Aristotle's philosophical term *telos,* final purpose, "that for the sake of which" something exists or an action is done. It refers to a longer, more distanced (tele-phone, tele-vision) perspective. If the final purpose of aging is character, then character finishes life, polishes it into a more lasting image. A Greek epitaph says: "I, who was such, am now a slab, a tomb, a stone, an image."[1] What is left after you have left is your being epitomized in images, especially the images toward the close, when so much has been stripped down and the finish of your character becomes more apparent as that peculiarly unique you. "Our distinction and glory," wrote Santayana, "as well as our sorrow, will have lain in being something particular."[2]

That particularity is given with our biological substance. Variety is more than the spice of life; variety is its truth. We ought never forget that we are each a different being. As the eminent Harvard biologist Richard Lewontin writes: "Indeed, no two unrelated humans who have ever lived or ever will live are likely to be identical even for the handful of commonest molecular polymorphisms."[3]

"Our greatest endeavour must be to make ourselves irreplaceable. . . ." said the Spanish philosopher Miguel de Unamuno (1864–1936); "no one else can fill the gap that will be left when we die." This is how to cross the finish line:

> For in fact each man is unique and irreplaceable; there cannot be any other I; each one of us—our soul, that is, not our life— is worth the whole Universe. . . . And to act in such a way as to make our annihilation an injustice, in such a way as to make our brothers, our sons, and our brothers' sons, and their son's sons, feel that we ought not to have died, is something within the reach of all.
>
> All of us, each one of us, can and ought to give as much of himself as he possible can—nay, to give more than he can, to exceed himself, to go beyond himself, to make himself irreplaceable.[4]

Where Unamuno gives nobility to the passion for uniqueness, Yeats's "Prayer for Old Age" adds to the passion a note of tragic humility, the irony of self-recognition: "I pray . . . that I may seem, though I die old, / A foolish, passionate man."[5]

The discipline demanded by Unamuno's charge goes beyond a final Herculean wrestle with old age and death. To make oneself irreplaceable is more than a spiritual exercise. It is aesthetic. The words "irreplaceable" and "unique" can as well be said of a painting, a poem, a dance performance. Each work of art is centered on itself and eccentric to all others. "There cannot be any other" than that single one.

That uniqueness is reflected in the stuff left on the dresser, the reading glasses on the nightstand, the trivial accumulations in the desk drawer that no one knows what to do with but are handed down as "valuables." Useless irrelevancies, yet now imbued with the specialness of art objects. Does the irreplaceable soul of the deceased pass into these ordinary bits of matter?

Is our image located only in the memory of those who remember us? Or does character remain in the objects collected, the tools used, the places inhabited? Perhaps history lives in the world's memory beyond human rememberings.

Jung said that after his wife died he was struck with a pang when he accidentally brushed by something of hers in the rooms they had shared. Did he project onto the object, or did the object reach out to him? The little things left are more than relics of the past, symbols of loss and mourning, transitional objects standing in for what has left. The departure of their living companion has transferred to them some of that former life, moving them from profane to sacred, from thing to image, from useful gadget to useless art. Like icons of the old Russian Orthodox church, they are now embodiments of soul, suddenly arrived at the aesthetic stature of "old."

The aesthetic finish calls up an image of genteel elders passing serenely away. This is not at all what I mean by "aesthetics." The word roots itself in a gasp (*aisthou*), a sudden short intake of breath in the face of wonder, or horror.[6] Aesthetics begins in the startle of surprise, the breath caught, held in astonishment. Aesthetics arises from an epiphanic image, the full force of character revealed as in a work of art.

Can a person become an epiphany? Can we entertain the idea that all along our earthly life has been phenomenal, a showing, a presentation? Can we imagine that at the essence of human being is an insistence upon being witnessed—by others, by gods, by the cosmos itself—and that the inner force of character cannot be concealed from this display. The image will out, and the last years put the final finish to the image.

It is then only natural that we become more like apparitions, already sepulchral effigies, stand-ins for ancestors. Visits to us become ceremonies; gifts, offerings; conversations, liturgical repetitions. We are left as traces, lasting in our very thinness like the scarcely visible lines on a Chinese silkscreen, microlayers of pigment and carbon, which can yet portray the substantial profundities of a face. Lasting no longer than a little melody, a unique composition of disharmonious notes, yet echoing long after we are gone. This is the thinness of our aesthetic reality, this old, very dear image that is left and lasts.

Notes

A PREFACE FOR THE READER

1. Lynn, Margulis (with Dorian Sagan), "Stamps and Small Steps: The Origin of Life and Our Cells," *Netview: Global Business News* (August 3, 1997), p. 3.
2. Theodore Roszak, *America the Wise: The Longevity Revolution and the True Wealth of Nations* (New York: Houghton Mifflin, 1998), p. 240.
3. Ibid., p. 248.
4. T. S. Eliot, *Four Quartets* (London: Faber & Faber, 1944), II.5.
5. José Ortega y Gasset, *The Origin of Philosophy,* Toby Talbot, trans. (New York, London: W. W. Norton & Co., 1967), pp. 62–63.
6. Alfred North Whitehead, *Modes of Thought* (New York: Capricorn Books, 1958), p. 50.

A PREFACE FROM THE WRITER

1. George Rosen, *Madness in Society* (London: Routledge & Kegan Paul, 1968), p. x.
2. C. G. Jung, *Letters,* vol. 1, G. Adler and A. Jaffé, eds. (Princeton, N.J.: Princeton University Press, 1973), p. 516.
3. Eliot, *Four Quartets,* II.2.
4. Kathleen Woodward, *At Last, the Real Distinguished Thing: The Late Poems of Eliot, Pound, Stevens, and Williams* (Columbus: Ohio State University Press, 1980), p. 122.
5. David Mamet, quoted in "Fortress Mamet," by John Lahr, *The New Yorker* (November 17, 1997), p. 82.
6. Don DeLillo, quoted in "Exile on Main Street," by David Remnick, *The New Yorker* (September 15, 1997), p. 47.

7. Maurice Blanchot, *The Writing of the Disaster,* Ann Smock, trans. (Lincoln and London: University of Nebraska Press, 1995), p. 10.

8. Woody Allen, *Without Feathers* (New York: Random House, 1975), p. 102.

9. Baruch Spinoza, *Ethics,* IV (London: Everyman's Library, 1910), p. 187.

A PREFACE TO THE BOOK

1. Friedrich Nietzsche, *Beyond Good and Evil,* Helen Zimmer, trans. (Edinburgh: Foulis, 1911), pp. 211–12.

CHAPTER 1: LONGEVITY

1. Plato, *Sophist,* in *Plato's Theory of Knowledge,* Francis MacDonald Cornford, trans. (London: Kegan Paul, Trench, Trubner & Co., 1946), pp. 245D–255E.

2. Steven Pinker, *How the Mind Works* (New York: W. W. Norton, 1997), p. 21.

3. Aristotle, *The Works of Aristotle,* J. A. Smith and W. D. Ross, trans. (Oxford: Clarendon Press). Cf. Troy Wilson Organ, *An Index to Aristotle* (New York: Gordian Press, 1966), "soul."

4. Richard Feynman, *What Do You Care What Other People Think?* (New York: Bantam, 1998), p. 244.

5. Steven M. Albert, Maria G. Cattell, and Albert Cattell, *Old Age in Global Perspective: Cross-Cultural and Cross-National Views* (New York: G. K. Hall & Co., 1994), p. 161.

6. Ibid., p. 163.

7. Ibid., pp. 225–27.

8. Ibid., p. 230.

9. Plato, *Republic,* Paul Shorey, trans., in *Plato: The Collected Dialogues,* Edith Hamilton and Huntington Cairns, eds., Bollingen Series 71 (New York: Pantheon, 1961), p. 329d.

10. Cicero, *De Senectute,* W. A. Falconer, trans. (London: Wm. Heinemann, 1930), p. 17.

11. Thomas Browne, *Religio Medici* (London: Everyman, 1964), p. 47.

12. Simone de Beauvoir, *The Coming of Age,* Patrick O'Brian, trans. (New York: G. P. Putnam's Sons, 1972), p. 454.

13. T. S. Eliot, "Ash Wednesday," in *Collected Poems of T. S. Eliot* (New York: Harcourt Brace and Co., 1936).

14. Robert Bly, "My Father at Eighty-Five," in *Meditations on the Insatiable Soul* (New York: Harper Collins, 1994), pp. 30–32.
15. Saul Kent, *Life Extension Magazine* (August 1998), p. 7.
16. *Foresight Update* 27:4 (Palo Alto, Calif.: Foresight Institute, 1996), p. 30.
17. *Fortune* (December 9, 1996), p. 3.

CHAPTER 2: THE LAST TIME

1. Eliot, *Four Quartets,* II.
2. Ezra Pound in *Imagist Poetry,* Peter Jones, ed. (London: Penguin, 1972), pp. 32–41.
3. Philip Hamburger, "Al Hirschfeld Blows Out His Candles," *The New Yorker* (June 22/29, 1998), p. 42.
4. W. B. Yeats, "A Dialogue of Self and Soul," in *The Collected Poems of W. B. Yeats* (London: Macmillan, Ltd., 1952), p. 267.
5. C. G. Jung, *Memories, Dreams, Reflections,* recorded and edited by Aniela Jaffé, Richard and Clara Winston, trans. (London: Collins & Routledge, 1963), p. 330.

CHAPTER 3: OLD

1. Ashley Crandell Amos, "Old English Words for *Old,*" in *Aging and the Aged in Medieval Europe,* Michael M. Sheehan, ed. (Toronto: Pontifical Institute of Mediaeval Studies, 1990), p. 103.
2. Ibid., 104.
3. Virginia Woolf, *The Death of the Moth and Other Essays* (New York: Harcourt Brace Jovanovich, 1970), p. 204.
4. John T. Wortley, "Aging and the Desert Fathers: The Process Reversed," in *Aging and the Aged in Medieval Europe,* pp. 63–74.
5. Amos, p. 101.
6. Eliot, *Four Quartets,* II.5.
7. Robert Young, *Analytical Concordance to the Bible* (London: Society for Promoting Christian Knowledge, n.d.), pp. 713–14.

CHAPTER 4: FROM "LASTING" TO "LEAVING"

1. Roger Gosden, *Cheating Time: Sex, Science, and Aging* (London: Macmillan, 1996) p. 101.
2. Zhores Medvedev, "An Attempt at a Rational Classification of Theories of Aging," *Biological Reviews* 65 (1990), pp. 375–98.

3. Avram Goldstein, quoted in "Annals of Addiction," by Abraham Verghese, *The New Yorker* (February 16, 1998), p. 49.
4. Friedrich Nietzsche, "Thus Spake Zarathustra," in *The Philosophy of Nietzsche* (New York: Modern Library, n.d.), p. 33.

CHAPTER 5: REPETITION

1. Gilles Deleuze, *Difference and Repetition,* Paul Patton, trans. (New York: Columbia University Press, 1998), p. 1.
2. Søren Kierkegaard, *Repetition,* Walter Lowrie, trans. (New York: Harper Torchbooks, 1964), p. 34.
3. Barry Lopez, *Crow and Weasel* (San Francisco: North Point Press, 1990), p. 48.

CHAPTER 6: GRAVITY'S SAG

1. Eliot, "The Love Song of J. Alfred Prufrock," in *Collected Poems of T. S. Eliot.*

CHAPTER 7: WAKING AT NIGHT

1. "Why Do Men Urinate at Night?" *Harvard Men's Health Watch* (February 1998), pp. 5–6.
2. William Stafford, "A Ritual to Read to Each Other," in *Stories That Could Be True* (New York: Harper & Row, 1977), p. 52.

CHAPTER 10: MEMORY: SHORT-TERM LOSS, LONG-TERM GAIN

1. Sherwin B. Nuland, *How We Die: Reflections on Life's Final Chapter* (New York: Vintage Books, 1995), pp. 55–56.
2. Eliot, *Four Quartets,* III.2.
3. W. B. Yeats, "Byzantium," p. 281.

CHAPTER 11: HEIGHTENED IRRITABILITY

1. Fielding H. Garrison, *An Introduction to the History of Medicine,* 4th ed. (Philadelphia: W. B. Saunders, 1929), p. 318.
2. Natalie Angier, "How Dangerous to the Heart is Anger?" *The New York Times* (February 10, 1993), p. C12.
3. Dylan Thomas, "Do Not Go Gentle into That Good Night," in *Collected Poems 1934–1952* (London: J. M. Dent & Sons, 1964), p. 116.

CHAPTER 13: EROTICS

1. Raymond Klibansky, Erwin Panofsky, and Fritz Saxl, *Saturn and Melancholy: Studies in the History of Natural Philosophy Religion and Art* (London: Thomas Nelson & Sons, 1964), p. 35.
2. Ibid., p. 36.
3. Ibid., p. 17.
4. Ibid., p. 22.
5. C. D. O'Malley and J.B. de C.M. Saunders, *Leonardo on the Human Body* (New York: Henry Schuman, 1952), p. 461.
6. Roger Gosden, "Cheating Time," *World Review* (July 2, 1996), p. 4.
7. Samuel Atkin and Adam Atkin, "On Being Old," in *How Psychiatrists Look at Aging,* George H. Pollock, ed. (Madison, Conn.: International Universities Press, 1992), pp. 1–24.
8. Gosden, "Cheating Time," p. 3.
9. W. B. Yeats, "The Spur," p. 359.
10. Alasdair D. F. Macrae, *W. B. Yeats: A Literary Life* (New York: St. Martin's Press, 1995), p. 120.
11. Quotes from Yeats's poems "Sailing to Byzantium," "The Tower," and "After Long Silence" are from *The Collected Poems of W. B. Yeats.*
12. Justin Kaplan, *Walt Whitman: A Life* (New York: Simon & Schuster, 1980), pp. 47, 52.
13. Roger Asselineau, *The Evolution of Walt Whitman: The Creation of a Personality* (Cambridge, Mass.: The Belknap Press of Harvard University Press, 1960), p. 268.
14. Walt Whitman, "Ventures on an Old Theme" (from *Notes Left Over*), in *Complete Poetry and Collected Prose* (New York: The Library of America, 1982), p. 1055.
15. The sources for the anecdotes regarding female eroticism are as follows. Moreau: Marianne Gray, *La Moreau: A Biography of Jeanne Moreau* (New York: Penguin Books, 1996), pp. 225, 184; Neel: Patricia Hills, *Alice Neel* (New York: Harry N. Abrams, 1983), p. 130; Wood: Garth Clark, "Beatrice Wood," *Crafts* 153 (July/August 1998); Nin: Deirdre Bair, *Anaïs Nin: A Biography* (New York: Penguin, 1996); Sarton: Margot Peters, *May Sarton: A Biography* (New York: Alfred A. Knopf, 1997), p. 355; Dinesen: Judith Thurman, *Isak Dinesen: The Life of a Storyteller* (New York: St. Martin's Press, 1982), p. 352.
16. Emily Vermeule, *Aspects of Death in Early Greek Art and Poetry*

(Berkeley and Los Angeles: University of California Press, 1979), pp. 173–74.

17. William James, "The Will to Believe," in *Writings 1878–1899* (New York: The Library of America, 1992), p. 555.

18. Winifred Milius Lubell, *The Metamorphosis of Baubo: Myths of Woman's Sexual Energy* (Nashville, Tenn.: Vanderbilt University Press, 1994), pp. 39–40.

19. C. Kerényi, *Eleusis: Archetypal Image of Mother and Daughter* (New York: Bollingen Foundation, 1967), p. 40.

20. Pausanias, *Description of Greece*, J. G. Frazer, trans. (New York: Biblo and Tanner, 1965), III.18.1, II.32.3.

21. Wortley, p. 67; Violet MacDermott, *The Cult of the Seer in the Ancient Middle East* (Berkeley: University of California Press, 1971), pp. 71–77.

22. *Harvard Health Letter,* 23/8 1998, p. 5.

23. Alphonso Lingis, "Lust," in *Abuses* (Berkeley: University of California Press, 1994).

24. C. G. Jung, *The Collected Works of C. G. Jung,* R.F.C. Hull, trans., Bollingen Series XX (Princeton, N.J.: Princeton University Press).

CHAPTER 14: ANESTHESIA

1. *Wellness Letter,* University of California, Berkeley (October 1998), p. 5.

2. Robert Butler in *Aging and the Elderly: Humanistic Perspectives in Gerontology,* Stuart F. Spiker, Kathleen M. Woodward, and David D. Van Tassel, eds. (Atlantic Highlands, N.J.: Humanities Press, 1978), p. 391.

3. Whitehead, p. 28.

4. Yoel Hoffman, *Japanese Death Poems* (Rutland, Vt.: Charles E. Tuttle Co., 1986), pp. 157, 277, 278.

5. Butler, "Afterword," in *Aging and the Elderly,* p. 390.

6. W. B. Yeats, "Sailing to Byzantium," p. 217.

CHAPTER 15. HEART FAILURE

1. William Harvey, "Anatomical Dissertation," quoted in *The Discovery of the Circulation of the Blood,* by Charles Singer (London: Dawson, 1956), pp. 1–2.

2. Emile R. Mohler, quoted in "Bony Growths Found in Heart Valves," by N. Seppa, *Science News* (April 4, 1998), p. 212.

3. Augustine of Hippo, *The Confessions,* E. B. Pusey, trans. (New York: Dutton, Everyman's Library, 1966), 10.3.

4. Augustine of Hippo, *Enarrationes in Psalmos,* in *A Select Library of Nicene and Post-Nicene Fathers* (Grand Rapids, Mich.: Eerdmans Publishing Co.), XLII 12, XLI 8 (12).

5. Henry Corbin, *Creative Imagination in the Sufism of Ibn Arabi,* Ralph Manheim, trans. (Princeton, N.J.: Princeton University Press, 1969), pp. 221–46.

CHAPTER 16: RETURN

1. Plotinus, *Enneads,* Stephen MacKenna, trans. (Burdett, N.Y.: Larsen Publications, 1992), II.2.2; 2.1.

2. Beauvoir, pp. 460–61.

INTERLUDE: THE FORCE OF THE FACE

1. Herman Melville, *Moby-Dick* (Harmondsworth, England: Penguin, 1972), pp. 114–15.

2. Ibid., pp. 144–45.

3. Michael Ventura, "Fifty Bucks Naked," *LA Village View* (May 27–June 2, 1994), p. 5.

4. Joyce D. Nash, *What Your Doctor Can't Tell You About Cosmetic Surgery* (Oakland, Calif.: New Harbinger, 1995), p. 124.

5. Ibid., p. 194.

6. Emmanuel Levinas, *Justifications de l'éthique,* in *The Levinas Reader,* Seán Hand, ed. (Oxford: Basil Blackwell, 1989), p. 81.

7. Roland Barthes, "The Face of Garbo," in *A Barthes Reader,* Susan Sontag, ed. (New York: Noonday Press, 1982).

8. William James, *Talks to Teachers on Psychology: And to Students on Some of Life's Ideals* (London: Longmans, Green and Co., 1911), p. 75.

9. Whitehead, p. 29.

10. T. E. Hulme, *Speculations* (London: Routledge & Kegan Paul, 1936), p. 162.

11. James Elkins, *The Object Stares Back: On the Nature of Seeing* (New York: Simon & Schuster, 1996), p. 200.

12. Levinas, *Justifications de l'éthique,* p. 83.

13. Emmanuel Levinas, *Difficult Freedom,* Seán Hand, trans. (Baltimore: Johns Hopkins Press, 1990), p. 140.

14. Levinas, *Justifications de l'éthique,* p. 83.

15. Emmanuel Levinas, *Totality and Infinity,* Alphonso Lingis, trans. (Pittsburgh: Duquesne University Press, 1969), p. 201.

16. George Kunz, *The Paradox of Power and Weakness: Levinas and an Alternative Paradigm for Psychology* (Albany: State University of New York Press, 1998), p. 27.

17. *Service of the Synagogue: New Year* (London: Routledge & Kegan Paul, n.d.), p. 209.

18. Louis Ginzberg, *The Legends of the Jews,* Henrietta Szold, trans. (Philadelphia: Jewish Publications Society, 1954); Gershom Scholem, *Major Trends in Jewish Mysticism* (London: Thames & Hudson, 1955).

19. Levinas, *Totality and Infinity,* p. 201.

20. Eliot, "The Love Song of J. Alfred Prufrock."

21. Jean-Jacques Courtine and Claudine Haroche, *Histoire du Visage* (Paris: Rivages/Histoire, 1998).

22. Nanao Sakaki, "Break the Mirror," in *Break the Mirror* (San Francisco: North Point Press, 1987), p. 108.

23. Carolyn H. Smith, "Old-Age Freedom in Josephine Miles's Late Poems, 1974–79," in *Aging and Gender in Literature,* Anne M. Wyatt-Brown and Janice Rossen, eds. (Charlottesville: University Press of Virginia, 1993), p. 278.

24. Beauvoir, p. 299.

25. W. B. Yeats, "Before the World Was Made," p. 308.

26. Elkins, p. 182.

27. Levinas, *Justifications de l'éthique,* p. 81.

28. Hulme, p. 229.

CHAPTER 17: FROM "LEAVING" TO "LEFT"

1. W. B. Yeats, "Byzantium," p. 281.

2. C. Kerényi, *Zeus and Hera,* Christopher Holme, trans. (London: Routledge & Kegan Paul, 1975), pp. 128–31.

3. Pausanius, VIII.22.2.

4. George Ripley, "The Bosom Book," in *Collectanea Chemica* (London: Vincent Stuart, 1963), pp. 140–41.

5. Wallace Stevens, "To an Old Philosopher in Rome," in *The Collected Poems of Wallace Stevens* (New York: Alfred A. Knopf, 1978), pp. 508–10.

CHAPTER 18: CHARACTER PHILOSOPHIZED

1. Keith H. Basso, *Wisdom Sits in Places: Landscape and Language Among the Western Apaches* (Albuquerque: University of New Mexico Press, 1996), p. 79.
2. Ibid., p. 85.
3. Lucien Lévy-Bruhl, *How Natives Think,* Lillian A. Clare, trans. (Princeton, N.J.: Princeton University Press, 1926; 1985), pp. 140–41.

CHAPTER 19: THE CHARACTER OF VIRTUES,
OR CHARACTER MORALIZED

1. James, *Talks to Teachers on Psychology,* p. 75.
2. Ibid., p. 67.
3. William J. Bennett, *The Moral Compass* (New York: Simon & Schuster, 1995), pp. 12, 13; *The Book of Virtues* (Simon & Schuster, 1993), p. 12.
4. Edward O. Wilson, "The Biological Basis of Morality," *Atlantic Monthly* (April 1998), p. 64.
5. Eliot, *Four Quartets,* IV.2.

CHAPTER 20: CHARACTER IMAGINED

1. Albert, Cattell, and Cattell, p. 59.
2. Carolyn H. Smith, in *Aging and the Elderly: Humanistic Perspectives in Gerontology,* Stuart F. Spiker, Kathleen M. Woodward, and David D. Van Tassel, eds. (Atlantic Highlands, N.J.: Humanities Press, 1978), p. 278.

CHAPTER 21: GRAND PARENTING

1. Steven Rose, *Biology Beyond Determinism* (New York: Oxford University Press, 1998), p. 211.
2. Roszak, p. 247.
3. Daniel C. Dennett, *Darwin's Dangerous Idea* (New York: Simon & Schuster, 1995), pp. 347, 344, 348.
4. Roszak, p. 248.
5. Anne Baring and Jules Cashford, *The Myth of the Goddess* (London: Viking, 1991), pp. 259, 303, 394.

CHAPTER 23: THE VIRTUES OF CHARACTER

1. Horace B. English and Ava C. English, *A Comprehensive Dictionary of Psychological and Psychoanalytical Terms* (New York: David McKay, 1958), p. 83.
2. Amélie O. Rorty, "Characters, Persons, Selves, Individuals," in *Identities of Persons,* A. O. Rorty, ed. (Berkeley: University of California Press, 1976), pp. 301–23.

CHAPTER 24: FINISH

1. Richmond Lattimore, *Themes in Greek and Latin Epitaphs* (Urbana: University of Illinois Press, 1962), p. 174.
2. Georges Santayana, *Realms of Being* (New York: Scribner's, 1942), p. xiv.
3. Richard Lewontin, *Human Diversity* (New York: Scientific American Library, 1995), p. 42.
4. Miguel de Unamuno, *Tragic Sense of Life,* J. E. Crawford Flitch, trans. (New York: Dover Publications, 1954), pp. 269–70.
5. W. B. Yeats, "A Prayer for Old Age," p. 326.
6. R. B. Onians, *The Origins of European Thought About the Body, the Wind, the Soul, the World, Time and Fate* (Cambridge: Cambridge University Press, 1954), p. 75.

Bibliography

Abram, David. *The Spell of the Sensuous.* New York: Pantheon, 1996.

Albert, Steven M., Maria G. Cattell, and Albert Cattell. *Old Age in Global Perspective: Cross-Cultural and Cross-National Views.* New York: G. K. Hall & Co., 1994.

Allen, Woody. *Without Feathers.* New York: Random House, 1975.

Amos, Ashley Crandell. "Old English Words for *Old.*" In *Aging and the Aged in Medieval Europe,* Michael M. Sheehan, ed. Toronto: Pontifical Institute of Mediaeval Studies, 1990.

Angier, Natalie. "How Dangerous to the Heart Is Anger?" *The New York Times,* February 10, 1993.

Aristotle. *The Works of Aristotle.* J. A. Smith and W. D. Ross, trans. Oxford: Clarendon Press.

Asselineau, Roger. *The Evolution of Walt Whitman: The Creation of a Personality.* Cambridge, Mass.: The Belknap Press of Harvard University Press, 1960.

Atkin, Samuel, and Adam Atkin. "On Being Old." In *How Psychiatrists Look at Aging,* George H. Pollock, ed. Madison, Conn.: International Universities Press, 1992.

Augustine of Hippo. *The Confessions.* E. B. Pusey, trans. New York: Dutton, Everyman's Library, 1966.

———. *Enarrationes in Psalmos* [Expositions of the Psalms]. In *A Select Library of Nicene and Post-Nicene Fathers.* Grand Rapids, Mich.: Eerdmans Publishing Co.

Bair, Deirdre. *Anaïs Nin: A Biography.* New York: Penguin, 1996.

Baring, Anne, and Jules Cashford. *The Myth of the Goddess.* London: Viking, 1991.

Barthes, Roland. *A Barthes Reader,* Susan Sontag, ed. New York: Noonday Press, 1982.

Basso, Keith H. *Wisdom Sits in Places: Landscape and Language Among the*

Western Apaches. Albuquerque: University of New Mexico Press, 1996.

Bataille, Georges. *Eroticism.* Mary Dalwood, trans. London and New York: Marion Boyars, 1987.

Beauvoir, Simone de. *The Coming of Age.* Patrick O'Brian, trans. New York: G. P. Putnam's Sons, 1972.

Bennett, William J. *The Book of Virtues.* New York: Simon & Schuster, 1993.

———. *The Moral Compass.* New York: Simon & Schuster, 1995.

Bergson, Henri. *Time and Free Will: An Essay on the Immediate Data of Consciousness.* F. L. Pogson, trans. New York: Harper Torch-books, 1960.

Blanchot, Maurice. *The Writing of the Disaster.* Ann Smock, trans. Lincoln and London: University of Nebraska Press, 1995.

Bly, Robert. *Meditations on the Insatiable Soul.* New York: Harper-Collins, 1994.

———. "Recognizing the Image as a Form of Intelligence," *Field* 24 (Spring 1981).

Brophy, John. *The Human Face Reconsidered.* London: George Harrap, 1962.

Browne, Thomas. *Religio Medici.* London: Everyman, 1964.

Budge, E. A. Wallis. *The Book of the Dead—The Chapters of Coming Forth by Day.* London: Kegan Paul, 1898.

Cannon, Walter B. *The Wisdom of the Body.* New York: Norton, 1932.

Cicero. *De Senectute.* W. A. Falconer, trans. London: Wm. Heinemann, 1930.

Clark, Garth. "Beatrice Wood." *Crafts* 153 (July/August 1998).

Clark, R. T. Rundle. *Myth and Symbol in Ancient Egypt.* London: Thames & Hudson, 1959.

Connery, Brian A. "Self-Representation and Memorials in the Late Poetry of Swift." In *Aging and Gender in Literature,* Anne M. Wyatt-Brown and Janice Rossen, eds. Charlottesville: University Press of Virginia, 1993.

Corbin, Henry. *Creative Imagination in the Sufism of Ibn Arabi.* Ralph Manheim, trans. Princeton, N.J.: Princeton University Press, 1969.

———. *Spiritual Body and Celestial Earth: From Mazdean Iran to Shi'ite Iran.* Nancy Pearson, trans. Princeton, N.J.: Princeton University Press, 1977.

Courtine, Jean-Jacques, and Claudine Haroche. *Histoire du Visage.* Paris: Rivages/Histoire, 1998.

Deleuze, Gilles. *Difference and Repetition.* Paul Patton, trans. New York: Columbia University Press, 1998.

DeLillo, Don. Quoted in "Exile on Main Street," by David Remnick, *The New Yorker,* September 15, 1997.

Dennett, Daniel C. *Darwin's Dangerous Idea.* New York: Simon & Schuster, 1995.

Eliade, Mircea. *Shamanism: Archaic Techniques of Ecstasy.* Willard Trask, trans. London: Routledge & Kegan Paul, 1964.

Eliot, T. S. *Collected Poems of T. S. Eliot.* New York: Harcourt, Brace & Co. 1936.

———. *Four Quartets.* London: Faber & Faber, 1944.

Elkins, James. *The Object Stares Back: On the Nature of Seeing.* New York: Simon & Schuster, 1996.

Emerson, Ralph Waldo. "Old Age" and "Character." In *The Works of Ralph Waldo Emerson,* vol. 3. New York: Harper & Brothers, n.d.

English, Horace B., and Ava C. English. *A Comprehensive Dictionary of Psychological and Psychoanalytical Terms.* New York: David McKay, 1958.

Erikson, Erik H. *The Life Cycle Completed: A Review.* New York: W. W. Norton & Co., 1982.

Euripides. *The Bacchae.* In *An Anthology of Greek Tragedy,* Charles Boer, trans.; Albert Cook and Edwin Dolin, eds. Indianapolis: Bobbs-Merrill, 1972.

Fenichel, Otto. *The Psychoanalytic Theory of Neurosis.* New York: W. W. Norton & Co., 1945.

Ferguson, John. *Moral Values in the Ancient World.* London: Methuen, 1958.

Feynman, Richard. *What Do You Care What Other People Think?* New York: Bantam, 1998.

Fierz-David, Linda. *Women's Dionysian Initiation.* Dallas: Spring Publications, 1988.

Foresight Update 27:4. Palo Alto, Calif.: Foresight Institute, 1996.

Fortune, December 9, 1996.

Fredrickson, George M. *The Inner Civil War.* Urbana: University of Illinois Press, 1993.

Freedberg, David. *The Power of Images.* Chicago and London: University of Chicago Press, 1989.

Garrison, Fielding H. *An Introduction to the History of Medicine,* 4th ed. Philadelphia: W. B. Saunders, 1929.

Ginzberg, Louis. *The Legends of the Jews,* vols. 1 and 2. Henrietta Szold, trans. Philadelphia: Jewish Publications Society, 1954.

Gray, Marianne. *La Moreau: A Biography of Jeanne Moreau.* New York: Penguin Books, 1996.

Goldstein, Avram. As quoted in "Annals of Addiction," by Abraham Verghese, *The New Yorker,* February 16, 1998.

Gosden, Roger. *Cheating Time: Sex, Science and Aging.* London: Macmillan, 1996.

———. "Cheating Time," *World Review,* July 2, 1996.

Hamburger, Philip. "Al Hirschfeld Blows Out His Candles." *The New Yorker,* June 22/29, 1998.

Harvard Health Letter 23/8, 1998.

Henry, Kimberly A., M.D., and Penny Keckaman. *The Plastic Surgery Handbook.* Los Angeles: Lowell House, 1997.

Heraclitus. *Ancilla to the Pre-Socratic Philosophers.* Kathleen Freeman, trans. Oxford: Basil Blackwell, 1948.

Hillman, James. "The Animal Kingdom in the Human Dream." In *Eranos Yearbook* 51 (1982). Frankfurt am Main: Insel Verlag, 1983.

———. "Concerning the Stone: Alchemical Images of the Goal." In *Sphinx* 5. London: The London Convivium for Archetypal Studies, 1993.

———. "Egalitarian Typologies Versus the Perception of the Unique." In *Eranos Yearbook* 45 (1976). Ascona, Switzerland: Eranos Foundation, 1980.

———. "On the Necessity of Abnormal Psychology." In *Facing the Gods,* James Hillman, ed. Woodstock, Conn.: Spring Publications, 1991.

Hills, Patricia. *Alice Neel.* New York: Harry N. Abrams, 1983.

Hoffman, Yoel. *Japanese Death Poems: Written by Zen Monks and Haiku Poets on the Verge of Death.* Rutland, Vt.: Charles E. Tuttle Co., 1986.

Hogrefe, Jeffrey. *O'Keeffe: The Life of an American Legend.* New York: Bantam, 1992.

Hulme, T. E. *Speculations.* London: Routledge & Kegan Paul, 1936.

James, William. *Writings 1878–1899.* New York: The Library of America, 1992.

———. *Talks to Teachers on Psychology: And to Students on Some of Life's Ideals.* London: Longmans, Green and Co., 1911.

Jones, Peter, ed. *Imagist Poetry.* London: Penguin, 1972.

Joyce, James. *Ulysses.* New York: Modern Library, 1934.

Jung, C. G. *Letters,* vol. 1, G. Adler and A. Jaffé, eds. Princeton, N.J.: Princeton University Press, 1973.

———. *Memories, Dreams, Reflections.* Recorded and edited by Aniela Jaffé. Richard and Clara Winston, trans. London: Collins & Routledge, 1963.

———. *The Collected Works of C. G. Jung,* vols. 6, 8, 13. R. F. C. Hull, trans., Bollingen Series XX. Princeton, N.J.: Princeton University Press, 1960–71.

Kaplan, Justin. *Walt Whitman: A Life.* New York: Simon & Schuster, 1980.

Kent, Saul. In *Life Extension Magazine,* August 1998.

Kerényi, C. *Dionysos: Archetypal Image of Indestructible Life.* Ralph Manheim, trans. Princeton, N.J.: Princeton University Press, 1976.

———. *Eleusis: Archetypal Image of Mother and Daughter.* New York: Bollingen Foundation, 1967.

———. *The Heroes of the Greeks.* H. J. Rose, trans. London: Thames & Hudson, 1959.

———. *Zeus and Hera.* Christopher Holme, trans. London: Routledge & Kegan Paul, 1975.

Kierkegaard, Søren. *Repetition.* Walter Lowrie, trans. New York: Harper Torchbooks, 1964.

Kilpatrick, William, and Gregory and Suzanne M. Wolfe. *Books That Build Character: A Guide to Teaching Your Child Moral Values Through Stories.* New York: Simon & Schuster, 1994.

Kirk, Geoffrey S. "Old Age and Maturity in Ancient Greece." In *Eranos Yearbook* 40 (1971). Leiden: E. J. Brill, 1974.

Klibansky, Raymond, Erwin Panofsky, and Fritz Saxl. *Saturn and Melancholy: Studies in the History of Natural Philosophy Religion and Art.* London: Thomas Nelson & Sons, 1964.

Kselman, Thomas A. *Death and the Afterlife in Modern France.* Princeton, N.J.: Princeton University Press, 1993.

Kunz, George. *The Paradox of Power and Weakness: Levinas and an Alternative Paradigm for Psychology.* Albany: State University of New York Press, 1998.

Lattimore, Richmond. *Themes in Greek and Latin Epitaphs.* Urbana: University of Illinois Press, 1962.

Levinas, Emmanuel. *Difficult Freedom.* Seán Hand, trans. Baltimore: Johns Hopkins Press, 1990.

———. *The Levinas Reader,* Seán Hand, ed. Oxford: Basil Blackwell, 1989.

———. *Totality and Infinity.* Alphonso Lingis, trans. Pittsburgh: Duquesne University Press, 1969.

Lévy-Bruhl, Lucien. *How Natives Think.* Lillian A. Clare, trans. Princeton, N.J.: Princeton University Press, (1926) 1985 (with new introduction by editor).

Lewontin, Richard. *Human Diversity.* New York: Scientific American Library, 1995.

Lingis, Alphonso. *Abuses.* Berkeley: University of California Press, 1994.

Lopez, Barry. *Crow and Weasel.* San Francisco: North Point Press, 1990.

Lubell, Winifred Milius. *The Metamorphosis of Baubo: Myths of Woman's Sexual Energy.* Nashville, Tenn.: Vanderbilt University Press, 1994.

MacDermott, Violet. *The Cult of the Seer in the Ancient Middle East.* Berkeley: University of California Press, 1971.

Macrae, Alasdair D. F. *W. B. Yeats: A Literary Life.* New York: St. Martin's Press, 1995.

Mamet, David. Quoted in "Fortress Mamet," by John Lahr, *The New Yorker,* November 17, 1997.

Marcovich, M. *Heraclitus: Greek Text with a Short Commentary.* Merida, Venezuela: Los Andes University Press, 1967.

Medvedev, Zhores. "An Attempt at a Rational Classification of Theories of Aging." *Biological Reviews* 65 (1990).

Melville, Herman. *Moby-Dick.* Harmondsworth, England: Penguin, 1972.

Merleau-Ponty, Maurice. *The Primacy of Perception: And Other Essays on Phenomenological Psychology, the Philosophy of Art, History and Politics.* James M. Edie, ed. Evanston, Ill.: Northwestern University Press, 1964.

———. *The Visible and the Invisible.* Alphonso Lingis, trans. Evanston, Ill.: Northwestern University Press, 1968.

Miller, David L. "Red Riding Hood and Grandmother Rhea." In *Facing the Gods,* James Hillman, ed. Woodstock, Conn.: Spring Publications, 1991.

Mohler, Emile R., in N. Seppa, "Bony Growths Found in Heart Valves." *Science News,* April 4, 1998.

Nash, Joyce D. *What Your Doctor Can't Tell You About Cosmetic Surgery.* Oakland, Calif.: New Harbinger, 1995.

Nietzsche, Friedrich. *Beyond Good and Evil.* Helen Zimmer, trans. Edinburgh: Foulis, 1911.

———. *The Philosophy of Nietzsche.* New York: Modern Library, n.d.

Nuland, Sherwin B. *How We Die: Reflections on Life's Final Chapter.* New York: Vintage Books, 1995.

O'Malley, C. D. and J.B. de C.M. Saunders. *Leonardo on the Human Body.* New York: Henry Schuman, 1952.

Onians, R. B. *The Origins of European Thought About the Body, the Mind, the Soul, the World, Time and Fate.* Cambridge: Cambridge University Press, 1954.

Organ, Troy Wilson. *An Index to Aristotle.* New York: Gordian Press, 1966.

Ortega y Gasset, José. *The Origin of Philosophy.* Toby Talbot, trans. New York, London: W. W. Norton & Co., 1967.

Pausanias. *Description of Greece.* J. G. Frazer, trans. New York: Biblo and Tanner, 1965.

Peters, Margot. *May Sarton: A Biography.* New York: Alfred A. Knopf, 1997.

Pinker, Steven. *How the Mind Works.* New York: W. W. Norton, 1997.

Plato. *Plato's Theory of Knowledge.* Francis MacDonald Cornford, trans. London: Kegan Paul, Trench, Trubner & Co., 1946.

———. *The Republic.* In *Plato: The Collected Dialogues.* Paul Shorey, trans.; Edith Hamilton and Huntington Cairns, eds. Bollingen Series 71, New York: Pantheon, 1961.

Plotinus. *Enneads.* Stephen MacKenna, trans. Burdett, N.Y.: Larsen Publications, 1992.

Pound, Ezra. In *Imagist Poetry,* Peter Jones, ed. London: Penguin, 1972.

Riefenstahl, Leni. *Leni Riefenstahl: A Memoir.* New York: St. Martin's Press, 1992.

Ripley, George. *Collectanea Chemica.* London: Vincent Stewart, 1963.

Rorty, Amélie O. "Characters, Persons, Selves, Individuals." In *Identities of Persons.* A. O. Rorty, ed. Berkeley: University of California Press, 1976.

Rose, Steven. *Biology Beyond Determinism.* New York: Oxford University Press, 1998.

Rosen, George. *Madness in Society.* London: Routledge & Kegan Paul, 1968.

Roszak, Theodore. *America the Wise: The Longevity Revolution and the True Wealth of Nations.* New York: Houghton Mifflin, 1998.

Sakaki, Nanao. *Break the Mirror.* San Francisco: North Point Press, 1987.

Santayana, George. *Realms of Being.* New York: Scribner's, 1942.

Scholem, Gershom. *Major Trends in Jewish Mysticism.* London: Thames & Hudson, 1955.

Service of the Synagogue: New Year. London: Routledge & Kegan Paul, n.d.

Shapiro, David. *Autonomy and Rigid Character.* New York: Basic Books, 1981.

Singer, Charles. *The Discovery of the Circulation of the Blood.* London: Dawson, 1956.

Smith, Carolyn H. "Old-Age Freedom in Josephine Miles's Late Poems, 1974–79." In *Aging and Gender in Literature,* Anne M. Wyatt-Brown and Janice Rossen, eds. Charlottesville: University Press of Virginia, 1993.

Spiker, Stuart F., Kathleen M. Woodward, and David D. Van Tassel, eds. *Aging and the Elderly: Humanistic Perspectives in Gerontology.* Atlantic Highlands, N.J.: Humanities Press, 1978.

Spinoza, Baruch. *Ethics.* London: Everyman's Library, 1910.

Stafford, William. *Stories That Could Be True.* New York: Harper & Row, 1977.

Stevens, Wallace. *The Collected Poems of Wallace Stevens.* New York: Alfred A. Knopf, 1978.

Theophrastus. *Characters.* J. M. Edmonds, trans. Cambridge, Mass.: Harvard University Press, 1967.

Thomas, Dylan. *Collected Poems 1934–1952.* London: J. M. Dent & Sons, 1964.

Thurman, Judith. *Isak Dinesen: The Life of a Storyteller.* New York: St. Martin's Press, 1982.

Unamuno, Miguel de. *Tragic Sense of Life.* J. E. Crawford Flitch, trans. New York: Dover Publications, 1954.

University of California, Berkeley. "Wellness Letter," October 1998.

Ventura, Michael. "Fifty Bucks Naked," *LA Village View,* May 27– June 2, 1994.

Vermeule, Emily. *Aspects of Death in Early Greek Art and Poetry.* Berkeley and Los Angeles: University of California Press, 1979.

Whitehead, Alfred North. *Modes of Thought.* New York: Capricorn Books, 1958.

Whitman, Walt. *Complete Poetry and Collected Prose.* New York: The Library of America, 1982.

"Why Do Men Urinate at Night?" *Harvard Men's Health Watch,* February 1998.

Wilson, Edward O. "The Biological Basis of Morality." *Atlantic Monthly,* April 1998.

Wolfe, Thomas. *A Stone, a Leaf, a Door.* New York: Scribner's, 1945.

Woodward, Kathleen. *At Last, the Real Distinguished Thing: The Late Poems of Eliot, Pound, Stevens, and Williams and Other Essays.* Columbus: Ohio State University Press, 1980.

Woolf, Virginia. *The Death of the Moth and Other Essays.* New York: Harcourt Brace Jovanovich, 1970.

Wortley, John T. "Aging and the Desert Fathers: The Process Reversed." In *Aging and the Aged in Medieval Europe.* Michael M. Sheehan, ed. Toronto: Pontifical Institute of Mediaeval Studies, 1990.

Yeats, W. B. *The Collected Poems of W. B. Yeats.* London: Macmillan, 1952.

Young, Robert. *Analytical Concordance to the Bible.* London: Society for Promoting Christian Knowledge, n.d.

Index

abnormal psychology, 171, 183
adolescents, xiv, 4, 14, 40, 46,
    141–42
  in high school, 125–30
aesthetics, xv, 116–18, 138–39, 184,
    193–94, 200–202
afterlife, 26, 155, 156
ageism, xviii–xix
aging, xiii–xxiii, xxvi, 53–62, 155,
    175, 199
  behavior inappropriate to,
    192–95
  humanist study of, 56–57
  inmost nature in, 54–55
  instrumentalist approach to, 57
  intelligence of, 54, 57, 59–61
  intention in, 59–61, 62
  involution of, 59–60
  old vs., 40, 41, 45
  paradigm shift in, 53–55
  physiological, 54–59, 60–61
  psychological, 54, 55, 56–62
  research on, xvi, 14, 22–23,
    55–57, 185; *see also*
    gerontology
  rot and, 60–61, 62
  shocked awareness of, 146–47
  symptoms of, 57–59, 60
  theories of, 55–56, 162
agitation, muddled, 78–80
Albert, Steven M., 14

alchemy, 82–83
  philosophers' stone of, 160–61,
    162, 163
alethia, xxi
Allen, Woody, xxv–xxvi, 29
altruism, 55, 189
  radical, 142
ambition, 18, 19–22
  eagle as symbol of, 21–22
ambologera, 112
American Academy of Cosmetic
    Surgeons, 137
America the Wise (Roszak), xx
Amos, Ashley Crandell, 42
ancestors, xxiv, xxx, 9, 14, 17, 22,
    61, 77, 80, 110–11, 151, 202
  as guardian spirits, 96, 188
  in Japan, 68
  night rituals for, 76
  repetition and, 64, 65, 66
  return of, 70
  as singular character traits, 99
  totem, 15
Anderson, Maxwell, 31
anesthesia, 114–18
anima mundi (world soul), 182–83
Anne, Saint, 190
anxiety, 54, 65, 66, 73, 77, 104,
    157–58, 161
Apache, 170
Aphrodite, 95, 112

JAMES HILLMAN is a psychologist, scholar, international lecturer, and the author of more than twenty books, including *The Soul's Code, Re-Visioning Psychology, Healing Fiction, The Dream and the Underworld, Inter Views,* and *Suicide and the Soul.* A Jungian analyst and originator of post–Jungian "archetypal psychology," he has held teaching positions at Yale University, Syracuse University, the University of Chicago, and the University of Dallas, where he co-founded the Dallas Institute for the Humanities and Culture. After thirty years of residence in Europe, he now lives in Connecticut.

ABOUT THE TYPE

This book was set in Bembo, a typeface based on an old-style Roman face that was used for Cardinal Bembo's tract *De Aetna* in 1495. Bembo was cut by Francisco Griffo in the early sixteenth century. The Lanston Monotype Machine Company of Philadelphia brought the well-proportioned letter forms of Bembo to the United States in the 1930s.